THE TRUTH BEHIND THE UNIFORM

HELEN ELIZABETH

Disclaimer

I have tried to recreate events, locales and conversations from my memories of them. In order to maintain their anonymity in some instances I have changed the names of individuals and places, I may have changed some identifying characteristics and details such as physical properties, occupations and places of residence.

ISBN: 978-1096388265

ISBN 13

Copyright © 2019 by Helen Elizabeth

All rights reserved.

No part of this book may be reproduced in any form or by any electronic or mechanical means, including information storage and retrieval systems, without written permission from the author, except for the use of brief quotations in a book review.

DEDICATION

I dedicate this book to my two beautiful girls, without you both in my life I would not have the strength to continue to strive to be the best I can be, I do so to inspire you both and be the loving mother every child deserves.

You have shown me the true meaning of unconditional love and I am blessed each and everyday to be your mummy and watching you grow into the incredible girls you are. I love you more than you will ever know.

To my wonderful partner for always believing in me and loving me without conditions. I couldn't be happier and look forward to our future. I love you.

To all the honourable police officers, I had the pleasure to serve with many of you. It's officers like you that make a difference. You do an increasingly difficult job, the sacrifices you make are often tarnished by the bad officers and sadly taken for granted by the government, force and the public.

A special thank you to Jenine of Jenine Taylor photography for the lovely photographs.

CONTENTS

Dedication	1
Prologue	5
1. Why Mummy?	11
2. Is That Attempted Murder	25
3. Stolen Innocence	37
4. What's Volleyball?	46
5. She's Gone for Good	52
6. Playing For England	67
7. The Police Force	76
8. Police Racism	94
9. My Pride, Her Prejudice	108
10. Fresh Start	116
11. Unlawful Police	131
12. Police Manipulation	147
13. Police Prejudice	156
14. Abuse of position	166
15. Pre-Wedding Assault	173
16. Data Protection Breach	178
17. Sex Discrimination	198
18. Police Bullying	221
19. Impossible Decisions	228
20. Rising From The Ashes	254
About the Author	262
Acknowledgments	264

PROLOGUE

My name is Helen, I am 37 years old and I grew up in Salford but now live in Cheshire, England with my partner Alexander, our two beautiful daughters Nova 7yrs, Evelyn 11 months, and our family dog George.

I write this book a different person to the girl I'm talking about but you will see that in the end I don't believe anyone could go through life and be subjected to the life experiences I have, and still be the same person, and some would debate a sane person, but I live to tell my experiences somewhat tarnished, but with a strength and character of a once broken woman who used the light of her daughter to bring her back from the brink. Sometimes I wonder, did this life really happen to me? Then I see the physical scars and the memories are so clear I have no doubt that it did.

. . .

I often wonder about the kind of woman I would be had my life been different, but I try not to dwell on it, I can't change the past but I do have some control over the present and the future, and I intend to live in the moment of each and every day that I continue to be blessed with.

This is by no means an easy feat, as life continues we will inevitably encounter obstacles and troubles, but it's our mindset that allows us to overcome these difficulties and move forward to live our life the way we chose, though we may have to accept that life is never going to fulfil all of our dreams and expectations.

I am now a retired police officer, when I joined the police force in 2003 aged 21 years, I never envisaged being in a position where I would be writing a book about my negative experiences and the awful behaviours I witnessed within the police force, but here I am.

I've had more than my fair share of hard times and countless battles, not only with the police force and others, but with myself too, and those I feel are the hardest to overcome. I may not have known the reason why at the time, but every crisis is an opportunity to close one door, and open other doors of opportunities, to create new adventures and possibilities which we may not immediately be aware of or have even expected.

. . .

I now know why I've had my hard times and struggles and if it wasn't for them, I wouldn't be here to share my experiences with you today, I share them in the hope that I can inspire you, motivate you and maybe even comfort you, so you know you are not alone.

I will tell you now, there were times when I would sit and wonder why me? What have I done to deserve this? Especially in my younger years. When I saw no way out, no light flickering at the end of the tunnel. I wanted to give up, but I didn't, I kept fighting. Some battles took more out of me than others, but each and every one of them made me the woman I am today, and I write this proud to be her.

Throughout this book I will be sharing my story with you, from having been the victim of numerous crimes as a child, by an abusive mother, to being a victim of sexual assault aged 11 years and 18 years, an abusive marriage and a police career that saw me bullied for daring to speak up for others and myself. I always felt my insight having been a victim of crime and surviving would help me be a good empathic police officer and hopefully be someone who made dealing with such horrendous situations that little bit easier, even if it made a difference to just one person.

However, within weeks I saw the negative side within the force, which led me on a path of bullying, harassment and sex discrimination and concluded in me taking legal advice and taking the police force down the route of an employment tribunal. I will also detail the incidents I saw where police officers despicable behaviours towards members of the public were both, abuse of power and sometimes criminal.

Now don't get me wrong, the majority of the police officers I have worked with I have found to be decent human beings, however there are the small minority and it is a minority, that give the rest of us a bad name and those are the ones that make the public distrust officers and make an already tough job even tougher. That said there is no room for these people to be in such a position of power and abuse it.

So why am I sharing my story with you? My intention isn't to smear the police, they do an incredibly difficult job, but people need to know the truth, that although there are bad apples, there are more good officers that try to uphold the position of police officer in a high regard. I tried so hard to change things within the police force but continued to be met with walls, bullies and cover ups, they may welcome women into the force, however, it is still a man's world, a lot of the older ranking officers are still old school and don't believe there is a place for women in a police role.

Racism, sexism, homophobia is all prevalent within the forces, don't be fooled that it doesn't exist. There needs to be change and if I can't do it from the inside, I will endeavour to do it from the outside.

. . .

I have changed everyone's names and the name of the police force involved, all locations will be known as a variation of Sandford, this is the name we use for all locations when training to be a police officer. This is not to protect the police force in question, or the officers involved, it is to protect not only myself and my family, but the victims and the family of the officers involved. I do not trust the police, I have every reason they will try to smear my name and deny everything, but this is my truth and the truth behind the uniform.

WHY MUMMY?

"Arghhhhhhhhhh!" I'm screaming in agony, "No mummy, Noooooooooo!" nothing I said could stop the pain surging through my fingers, into my hands and up my arm, it felt like my whole body was in pain, I can't hold back the tears, as they flow freely from my eyes and down my cheeks, I feel the salty taste as they fall into my open mouth.

I'm screaming for her to stop but she will not take the hot iron off my fingers, it felt like forever but must have only been a second, but it was the most excruciating moment of my young life, she finally released me and I fell backwards on to the kitchen floor, my head hit the door and before I knew what was happening she pulled me up by the same arm and dragged me across the floor kicking and screaming to the kitchen sink, pulling my arm and putting my hand underneath the freezing cold running water.

. . .

"Arghhhhh", I'm screaming again, the pain is unbearable, I don't know which is worse the hot iron or the freezing cold water on the injury, "Stop it you little bitch, this will teach you for giving your sister food" and then she let me go, again I fell to the floor wriggling in agony, all could think about was the pain in my fingers.

"Why mummy? Why?" I cry but I was met with silence as she walked back into the living room, sat on the sofa, lit her cigarette and continued to watch her television programme.

What did I do to deserve this? Well, one form of punishment mum used was starving us, sending us to our room and not allowing us food all day, so when one of my siblings was being punished this way, I would often make a little extra whilst making our lunch or dinner and I would sneak it up to whomever was being punished that day.

Back in the 80's and 90's we didn't lock our front door, so I was able to sneak out of the back door in to the garden. I would open the back gate sneak through the alleyway that adjoined our house to our neighbour's. As I came to the front of the house I would crouch down underneath the living room window and slowly sneak to the front door.

I would open the front door as quietly as I could, this opened directly into the small hallway and the stairs were immediately in front. So I would tip toe up the stairs and into the bedroom giving the child being punished food, on this particular occasion it was my younger sister Sarah.

It was whilst I was sneaking back downstairs my mum opened the living room door and caught me with the plate that warranted todays punishment. I definitely learnt a lesson from this incident but not the one you would think, next time, no evidence...... no plate!

I still have a few small scars on my hand from this incident and similar incidents, it's hard to differentiate which scars came from which incidents, even the middle finger nail on my right hands grows funny from the iron incidents too.

Someone I was romantically involved with once didn't know where they came from but told me they were just as perfect as me, he said the same about my eye brows too, I think that was the first time I ever looked at the scars on my hand and smiled, I was 23.

You see I have a scar in my right eyebrow too, where no hair grows and the shape of each eyebrow is slightly different on the inside, I must have been about 10 years old when this incident took place.

My mum used to play bingo on a Tuesday and Thursday evening and always took one of us with her, I never really knew why she did so until many years later I found out this was one of her ways to cover for her meeting up with other men, but mostly we were happy to go as we were allowed a packet of crisps and a fizzy drink.

On this one particular occasion it wasn't my turn to go and I was so excited to play with one of my best friend's, my next-door neighbour Bob. We were playing in our neighbour Shirley's garden, she was an older lady and would often let us play in her front garden, she had a garage and Bob and I would often hide in there. I was hiding in there when I heard my mum shouting me, "HELEN…… HELEN".

The garage I was in was only next door but one so I could hear my mum shouting my name, I just didn't fancy getting punished for something at that moment in time, I was being a child and having fun, so I thought if I continued to hide I would be able to continue playing and have whatever punishment I'd be subjected to later or I would be in bed and she would forget by the next day.

"HELEN….. HELEN IF YOU DON'T GET HERE NOW YOU'LL KNOW ABOUT IT", my mum continued to shout and the sound was getting closer, then the garage door swung open and my mum found me.

"You are coming with me to bingo tonight" she said.

. . .

"But mummy… I don't want to, it's not my turn".

"Tough Shit" she said as she grabbed hold of my arm and began to pull me out of the garage, I resisted and pulled back, I fell out of her grip and fell on to the floor.

"Please mummy" I pleaded, just as Bob came up behind my mum I got myself up of the ground. My mum didn't see Bob behind her as she took hold of the garage door and swung it forward so it would hit me, the door hit me in the face, it was the side of the door that had the Yale latch on it and I was just the right height for the latch to hit me right on the brow bone.

I immediately closed my eyes put my hands to my face as I screamed in pain, when I opened my eyes seconds later I couldn't see through the blood, I remember Bob helping me clear my eyes from the blood and help walk me home, as we got into the house my mum was sat on the sofa with her cigarette and my Dad came running to me asking what had happened, through my sobs all I could mutter was "the garage door".

To most people I have always said it was an accident with the garage door as once you start telling people about one incident, they want to know more and I didn't fancy telling people the truth, so for years only the three of us ever knew. Bob used to ask me why I never told the truth but if I told the truth about that I would have to tell the truth about everything else and who would believe a child. Bob promised never to reveal my secret.

It wasn't just me who was subjected to my mum's abuse, but I did get the brunt of it, if I saw one of my siblings getting the blame for something I would quickly say it was me, the pain my mum subjected me to was terrible but it wasn't as bad as watching my siblings get punished and hurt, that I couldn't bear even at such a young age.

I recall my youngest sister Amy walking in to the living room from the kitchen with a packet of crisps, mum didn't allow us to have food, unless we asked her for it and she had given us permission, which wasn't very often, only when Dad was home would we be allowed such treats.

She would often indulge in crisps, chocolate and treats in front of us and ask us if we would like some, then laugh if we said yes and we wouldn't be allowed any, so the moment my mum noticed Amy walking in from the kitchen with the packet of crisps she immediately stood up, marched furiously over to Amy grabbed hold of her by the hair and dragged her further into the living room, "What are you doing with these?" mum shouted .

Amy's immediate reaction was to grab hold of her own hair with both hands to try and ease the pain and in doing so she dropped the packet of crisps on the floor. Amy was crying so much I don't think she could even hear what our mum was saying in order to answer her, so I jumped up and said "I said she could have them" and in a split second my mum loosened her grip on Amy who fell to the ground and in an instant her hand came and slapped me across the face, the stinging sensation was so intense but all I could do was kneel down on the floor and cuddle my little sister to console her, my mum however had other ideas.

I heard her say, "Pick them up" so I let go of my sister to do as mum asked and pick the crisps up, "Not you, her!" she snapped, so my little sister let go of me, walked over to the crisps and picked them up, she looked at our mum like the scared little six year old she was wondering what she was supposed to do.

Then our mum shouted "well bring them here then stupid" so Amy walked over tentatively to our mum and gave them to her, my mum told Amy to stand there, right in front of her and watch as our mum slowly began to eat the crisps, one by one whilst laughing and smirking at Amy, Amy began to cry and as our mum finished the crisps she told Amy they were nice and to put the empty packet in the bin. This was something our mum got considerable pleasure from.

My Dad was a biker and would go to work on his motorbike, even at such a young age I was always worried that he wouldn't come home safely, maybe it was because Dad had a previous accident and my Dad's biker friends often had accidents, even my Dad's closet friend who we called uncle Daz had an accident once and I remember him walking in to our home immediately after the accident laughing and holding his blooded hand up as he had lost the top of his index finger, then he said to my Dad I think I need a drink.

As Dad sometimes worked late night shifts, I would find myself so worried about him I couldn't sleep properly, but as soon as I heard his motorbike coming I knew he was home safely, and I could go to sleep. As I think back now and it's such an adult thing for a child so young to be worried about, yet to me it was natural.

This particular evening Dad was working a night shift and I was no older than 10, because there were four girls we all shared a bedroom and we had bunk beds, my oldest sister Emily and youngest sister Amy shared a bunk bed with Emily on the top bunk and Amy on the bottom, then the two middle sisters Sarah and I shared the other bunk bed with myself on the top bunk and Sarah on the bottom.

It must have been about 5:30am and I was woken by Amy and Sarah screaming and shaking me awake, as I woke I noticed the curtains on the main window of our bedroom were on fire, I immediately jumped out of bed and told my younger sister Amy to go and wake mum, as they ran in to our mum and Dad's bedroom I ran in to the bathroom and filled a jug of water, ran back in to our bedroom and threw it on the fire but it was nowhere near enough water, my oldest sister Emily was still in bed sleeping through all of the commotion, I ran back to the bathroom to find something bigger than the jug but I couldn't find anything.

I quickly put the plug in the bath and started to fill the bath up then ran out of the bathroom on to the landing and my two sisters came running out of my mum and Dad's bedroom crying because they couldn't wake mum. I remember telling them to stay with mum and keep trying to wake her and stay away from the fire in our bedroom.

I ran in to the kitchen I picked up the mop bucket and started filling it with water, I also put the washing up bowl in the sink and started to fill that, as the first one filled up I took it and ran upstairs and threw it on to the fire then I ran in to the bathroom and put that one in the bath to fill up whilst I ran downstairs to collect the other bucket, I ran back upstairs in to our bedroom and threw the mop bucket full of water on to the fire, at this point my eldest sister Emily had also woken and was in the bathroom getting the kitchen bowl from the bath and threw it on to the fire and with that the fire was out.

Mum had finally woke and came running in to the bedroom shouting at us and demanding to know what was going on, I told her there was a fire and we tried to wake her, she was furious and demanded to know what had happened. My two younger sisters started to cry again and handed a can of lighter fuel and a lighter over to our mum, they tried to explain that they were trying to fill up mum's lighters for her, she slapped them both across the face so hard they fell to the floor, crying hysterically and mum left our bedroom shouting "You'd better clean that up before your Dad gets home" as she went back to bed.

I immediately comforted my sisters who again tried to explain that they were sat on the floor between the two bunkbeds next to the window just trying to fill up our mum's lighters, and the next minute the curtains that were closed had caught fire. Once they stopped crying, we couldn't help but laugh at our older sister Emily who had not only slept through most of the incident but the head of her bed was next to the curtains and she was incredibly lucky that her hair or bedding had not caught fire, but her face did have black marks from the smoke.

We all tried to clean the room as best as we could but it wasn't possible to clean anything really, one side of the room that was pink was now black, the window was black as was the radiator and the curtains, well, there was hardly anything left of them.

Dad arrived home around 8:00 am and we were so scared to tell him what had happened. Our mum however told Dad what had happened and informed him that it was her who had been running around getting the water and putting the fire out. Needless to say, we were grounded.

My mum wasn't a maternal person in the slightest so even now it puzzles me as to why she had so many children.

One thing My mum loved to use to punish us with was her belt, I can recall almost every detail of this belt because we were made to go and get the belt when we were going to being punished this way. If we refused fetch it, it would be the closest thing to hand, a hairbrush, a shoe, a slipper, anything she could use to hit us with. The belt was a thick dark brown leather belt about three inches wide, the edges of the belt were a lighter brown due to wear and tear and it had an oval metal buckle with a picture of an eagle on it and the metal hook on the back that would hook into the hole to fasten the belt.

The belt itself had beautiful detailing imprinted on it, along with my mum's name in capital letters **H E L E N**.

When she would use the belt on us she would make us bend over her knee or the arm of the chair pull our trousers down and hit us so hard it would sometimes leave the imprint of the detailing on our bottoms, often we would have her name across our bottom, the worse times were if you were hit by the buckle or the hook, it was agony, not only because it broke our skin and caused bleeding, but our bottom would be so bruised we couldn't sit down properly for days and our mother didn't like us siting on the sofa so we would have to try to sit on a hard floor with a beaten bottom.

Like any young girl I loved dressing up, trying on my mother's shoes and clothes, putting on her makeup and dancing around her bedroom, I felt free, free to dance, free to pretend I was a princess, or a fairy and free to imagine I was someone else, even somewhere else, somewhere other than where I actually was, at home with my own wicked mother.

I loved doing this and I would often lose myself in my character and on this particular occasion I was in my mum and Dads bedroom pretending to be a childhood favourite of mine, Dorothy Gale from The Wizard Of OZ, I was following my own yellow brick road and my head was down looking at my " Ruby slippers" when in actual fact they were my mother's fuchsia pink and black stilettos heels, very 80's. I didn't hear my mum open the door and come in to the bedroom because I was also singing, "What are you doing?" she shouted.

I told her I was pretending to be Dorothy Gale and that I wanted to be an actress when I was older, I immediately knew I was in big trouble, she started laughing at me and told me I would never be an actress, "Why?" I asked. Her response is one I will never forget.

. . .

"You an actress? You are too fat and ugly to be an actress, no one will want you" she laughed.

Then she grabbed hold of my arm, pulled me round to face her whilst continuing to laugh and tell me I was too fat and ugly, I lost my balance and being 7 years old and in 5 inch stiletto's I couldn't regain my balance and I fell over, as I did, I grabbed hold of my mum to try and balance, unfortunately in doing so I ended up pulling her on to the floor with me, needless to say she was furious with me.

She got up, leaving me on the floor, took one of the stiletto shoes off my foot and proceeded to beat me with it. Luckily she was holding the heel so it was just the foot part that connected with my cowering body, she was hitting my bottom and legs that hard the heel broke off the shoe. She threw the shoe to the ground and shouted at me to leave her bedroom, I immediately got up and as I walked past her she struck me across the head and said "Take that shit off your face, you look like a tart".

So I went into the bathroom and washed the makeup off my face, I was relieved to hear her leave her bedroom and go downstairs. Once my face was cleaned I took my mums dress off and went in to my bedroom where I curled up on my bed, held my favourite teddy bear Snowy as tight as possible and burst into tears, asking snowy why? Why couldn't I have a nice mummy and I cried myself to sleep.

. . .

As children we expect our mummies and Daddies to be the people to protect us, build our confidence, tell us we are the most beautiful little girl in the world and encourage us to dream. They are the ones to help make us feel better when we're sad or hurt, yet up until that point no words had ever hurt me more than those words my mum said to me that day.

I couldn't stop thinking if my mummy thought I was fat and ugly I must be. I was used to being physically hurt by my mum and called stupid, a bitch, a little cow those kinds of names but those words that day, they haunted me for many years even long after my mother had left.

IS THAT ATTEMPTED MURDER

My Dad was the typical man in many ways, he really wanted a son so mum and Dad continued to get pregnant until they had a son. My mum unfortunately suffered two miscarriages one before me and one straight after so me so I already count my blessings to be here. So when my brother arrived in 1987 my Dad was elated to finally have a son. Jacob was born two months premature and suffered some initial complications at the hospital but all four of the girls were delighted when he came home, he was like our real-life dolly and we all doted on him, we took it in turns to feed him, help bathe him in the kitchen sink and dress him.

Mum however seemed to resent Jacob more than any of us girls, the reason I can only assume, was because my Dad wanted a son so much, this was evident from day one. When Dad wasn't home, Jacob was often left in a dirty nappy, mum didn't tend to him, she would sit on the sofa smoking, whilst watching tv.

When Jacob was around three he and I were upstairs playing in his bedroom when my mum came upstairs, she shouted at us to shut up as she headed past the bedroom, I don't know why I did, but I looked out of Jacob's bedroom to see where my mum had gone and she was in the bathroom, she was stood at the sink with her back to me and I watched as she took my brother's sippy cup and poured something in to it, she then put a little water from the tap in to it and then shouted me.

"Helen" she said "Helen, get your arse here".

So I went to the bathroom and asked my mum what she wanted, she held out her hand with my brother's sippy cup and asked me to go and give it to him, I asked her what was in the sippy cup and she slapped me across the face and said "none of your business", so I took hold of the sippy cup and went into my brothers bedroom and gave it to him. Just as I did, I heard the front door open and it was my Dad coming home from work, Jacob went to have some of his drink from the sippy cup, as I was leaving his room to see go my Dad, my mum stormed into the bedroom and shouted

"WHAT ARE YOU DOING YOU STUPID COW" she yelled.

. . .

I continued out of my brother's room as my Dad came running up the stairs to see what the commotion was all about, he passed by me saying "Hello Titch", Titch was my nickname off my Dad as between my mum and I, I was the smaller of the two Helen's, Dad went into my brother's bedroom and I followed, mum was walking towards the door to exit the bedroom when my Dad asked what was going on, my mum told my Dad she had just caught me giving my brother a sippy cup which she saw me fill with detergent in the bathroom and Jacob was just about to drink it, when mum realised what was happening she'd rushed in to stop Jacob from drinking it.

My Dad took hold of the sippy cup from my mum, opened it and was greeted by the fragrant aroma of the bathroom detergent, he looked at me with a look I had never witnessed from my Dad before, it was both disappointment and anger, I immediately started to cry and tried to explain that it wasn't me and that I had seen mum fill it up and she had given me the sippy cup to give to Jacob, mum continued to lie, telling my Dad what she allegedly saw me do and called me a liar, I was hysterical.

I could see my Dad was furious, he stormed out of my brother's bedroom with the sippy cup in hand not saying a word and went in to the bathroom where he poured the concoction down the sink, he then headed directly for me where he took hold of my arm and proceeded to smack my bottom, he hit me so hard, again and again and again, I was screaming at the top of my lungs .

"It wasn't me! No Daddy", I continued to scream with tears streaming down my face but he wouldn't stop, it felt like he was never going to stop then he left me on the landing floor, shouted something at me that I can't recall and walked off in to my brothers bedroom, I saw my other three sister standing on the stairs peeking through the rails to see what was happening upstairs, my Dad then walked past me with my brother and went downstairs with my mum following them.

I was still crying hysterically, curled up in the foetal position on the floor, I couldn't believe what had just happened, my Dad had never hit me like that before, I was used to beatings from my mum but not from my Dad, until this point the worst punishment I had ever had from him was a smacked bottom.

I felt sick from the shock and pain and I physically couldn't move. I don't know how long I was lying on the floor like this before I could finally muster the energy to move my body, but when I could I dragged myself across the landing floor. Slowly and painfully I managed to get to my bedroom, I pushed the door open, crawled to my bed and got into it.

. . .

I lay there crying, my whole body was aching from head to toe, it felt like even my heart was bruised, but I realised my heart was just breaking from what I had just experienced from my Dad. I took hold of Snowy, my trusty teddy bear, I pulled him in to my chest and cuddled him so tightly, if he was alive, I would have squeezed out his last breath. I didn't want to move, I didn't want to go downstairs and have dinner, at that moment I just wanted to forget, but my head kept replaying the incident over and over like an old movie reel.

At some point I fell asleep, when I woke up the next morning, I was in so much pain, I didn't want to get out of bed, my sister's beds were already empty, so I presumed they had already gone downstairs and then I heard my Dad call my name and tell me to get up and come downstairs.

With every inch of my body feeling like it was hurting I managed to get out of bed and go downstairs. My Dad had made me some toast for breakfast, he had put it on the kitchen table, and I went and sat at the table to eat my breakfast. The table had hard surface benches and as I sat tears filled my eyes, I don't recall if it was because of the physical pain or because I was so heartbroken, I looked up and I could see my Dad preparing some food on one of the kitchen counters, he didn't look at me or speak to me, but as he came in to my view I couldn't help the tears from running down my cheeks and tarnish my toast giving it that salty taste.

. . .

I saw my Daddy in a whole different light that morning, my Daddy was my hero, he made our childhood happy when he was home, but I couldn't even begin to say anything to him and he said nothing to me. We have never spoken about the incident but when I think about this day, I remember it as one of the worst days of my life.

My mum was a very lazy person, I don't recall her ever working a day in her life when we were children, even the house chores were done by our Dad or myself and my siblings, the only meal I can ever recall our mum making was Christmas dinner around 1991. Dad was a great cook but on this particular Christmas he was in bed very poorly which was very unusual for my Dad as he never seemed to get poorly, but he was so poorly he couldn't even manage to get himself out of bed.

I remember the barrage of verbal abuse my mum was shouting at him because she was left to cook the Christmas dinner. My Dad used to put the turkey in the oven in the early hours of Christmas morning and when we woke up on Christmas Day, we would smell the turkey slowly cooking, it is one of those amazing sensory memories whenever I smell turkey cooking.

On this occasion my Dad was just too poorly so my mum had to get the turkey ready, I was stood in the kitchen with mum as she was putting the turkey in the oven, I remember telling her she needed to put the foil around it like Dad and then take it off close to the end of cooking, she told me to fuck off and get out, so I did.

Christmas didn't feel the same without the smell of turkey and my Dad downstairs with us, I remember constantly popping up to see if he was ok and ask him to come down, but he was unable to.

We were all incredibly hungry and had managed to eat our way through our selection boxes all morning and lunch time, the next minute smoke was coming out of the kitchen and it was safe to say mum made sure the turkey was dead, in fact it was cremated, still she served dinner and it wasn't very nice, it was the worst Christmas dinner. Later that day my Dad managed to come downstairs as he felt a lot better.

Over the years I can't help but think if my mum had put something in one of my Dad's drinks the night before on Christmas Eve. Christmas Eve is my Dad's birthday, our granDad would always come round have some drinks to celebrate and stay over, we were allowed to stay up the older we got as one Christmas, Emily and I had caught my Dad and granDad doing the Father Christmas thing, so from then on we didn't have to go to bed very early and we could help put the presents out.

On this particular Christmas Eve I do recall my mum making my Dad some drinks which she never did, so I've always begged the question did my mum put something in my Dad's drink that made him so poorly…..Who knows?

I love the tradition we have in the UK, Fish and Chips Friday, I love Fish and Chips from the chippy, unfortunately in our house this tradition was one only enjoyed by our mum. One Friday Dad was working, and mum gave me a £20 note and told me to go to the local chip shop and get her favourite meal, chips, pudding, peas and gravy. I took the money and placed it in my coat pocket, then set off for the ten minute walk.

Once I got to the chip shop, I placed the order then reached inside my coat pocket to retrieve the money but I couldn't find it, the feeling I got in my stomach was one of pure dread of returning home to tell my mum what had happened, I told the lady at the chippy what had happened and that I needed to go and look for the money.

I set of to retrace my steps but I couldn't find the money, tears filled my eyes as I knew exactly what was going to happen when I returned home, I must have spent 30 minutes looking for the money but I couldn't find it anywhere.

I decided to head home and face the consequences. When I entered the front door, I took a deep breath before I went in to the living room to face my mum, as I entered she was sat

THE TRUTH BEHIND THE UNIFORM

in her favourite chair with her back to me, without looking at me my mum told me to get her a fork and plate.

"Mum…. I'm sorry, I lost the money" I said.

"Get out you stupid little bitch and find it now…. Don't come back without it" she replied.

"I've tried and can't find it anywhere mum…. I'm so sorry".

And with that my mum put her cigarette in the ashtray and launched at me, holding me with one hand whilst hitting me with the other. I tried so hard to hold the tears but my ten year old body hurt too much and I couldn't stop them from falling down my cheeks, my siblings were screaming and crying and then finally my mum stopped and shouted at us all to get out, I took hold of my two younger sisters and brother and we all ran up the stairs into our bedroom.

We all cuddled on my bed as I reassured my siblings, they were ok and to stop crying. I read them a couple of books and before long because we were so exhausted my siblings fell asleep, one by one I helped them all to their own beds and we all went to sleep with empty stomachs.

I don't want you to think my childhood was all bad

because it wasn't, when my Dad was home, we had some wonderful times. My Dad was a good man and when we were younger a great Dad, he was my hero. He made sure we had birthday parties and he made some great birthday cakes for us, I still recall the chocolate cake covered with smarties, it was so colourful I didn't want to spoil it by eating it and for my eleventh birthday I had two number one's, I made sure everyone else shared one number one and my Dad and I had the other number one.

He never let us down. I recall us going to the indoor market when I was a young child and at the toy stall we found a box of colourful swords with sheaths, I had a pink one and my Dad had an orange one and we began sword fighting in the middle of the market hall, we got so into it, we were moving in and out of the stalls laughing and having so much fun, fun which was then spoilt by the stall holder who had us thrown out of the market hall.

My Dad had motorbikes and we had a shed in our back garden and I remember us spending hours in the shed whilst my Dad was cleaning or tinkering with his motorbike, I was a young girl who enjoyed spending time with her Daddy no matter what we were doing.

We didn't have much money growing up, but my Dad made the most of everything, we always had birthday and Christmas presents they may not have been expensive, but we always had them, and he made any special occasion memorable for us.

We went all out at Christmas time; you could barely see the wallpaper for the amount of decorations and cards we had on the walls. We loved Christmas so much we even put the decorations up in late November, it really was the most magical time of the year and I have many a happy memory from Christmas time with my Dad

On a Sunday we used to go out for walks, Dad, Daz and my siblings. Our Sunday walks or adventures as they became known were legendary which made all the other children on the street regularly want to come with us.

We found something we called a "Moon Cave" and would often spend hours playing there, then returning home for one of our Dads Sunday roast dinners which were mouth wateringly delicious and then our Sunday evening bath, we took our bath's in order of age so youngest always went first. My favourite part about Sunday bath time was coming downstairs and having my Dad brush and dry our hair whilst we were watching "Bullseye".

On one of these adventures we had been walking for hours and we were lost, we found ourselves in the middle of a field. We were so hungry and couldn't help but moan about it, so my Dad bent down and pulled up a plant from out of the ground, wiped it clean and threw it at me and said, "Eat that". It was a huge carrot and before he could tell the others to pull themselves a carrot, they were all cleaning and chomping away on the carrots we had just unearthed.

As my Dad and Daz were eating their carrots and figuring out a plan, we heard someone shouting for us to "Get off his land before he shoots" we immediately all started to run, we had never ran so fast in our lives but in doing so as we climbed a fence to exit the field we found ourselves at a familiar road and Dad and Daz knew where we were.

As we stopped to catch our breath we couldn't help but laugh, as I turned around to see my siblings I laughed further because I noticed my brother despite his young age had run with his t-shirt folded from the bottom to his chest carrying his "Loot" he had a t-shirt full of carrots. So, as we set off home, we were all quietly munching away on our stolen carrots.

I have so many wonderful memories of my Dad and siblings as a child, times with our Dad was a real childhood, fun, laughter, joy, innocence everything that a child should be able to experience and I can genuinely sit back and smile fondly with a warm heart knowing that despite what my mother subjected us to we had a good childhood because of my Dad.

STOLEN INNOCENCE

It was a scorching hot June summers day, In the summer of 1993. Myself and one of my friends Matilda were excited to go to the summer fair on Sandford recreation ground known as 'Sandford Rec'. It was something that occurred every year only this year I was allowed to go on my own with my friend.

I was wearing my favourite red and white horizontal t-shirt and black cycling shorts, Matilda knocked on the front door and we went into the front garden, jumped on our pushbikes and got ready to go.

The living room windows were wide open as I was passing them and shouted

. . .

"Goodbye" to my Dad through the window, then I heard my Dad shout me

"TICH" he shouted

"Argh….. Yes Dad" I shouted

"Come here Kiddo" he replied.

I looked at Matilda and we both had that sinking feeling my Dad was changing his mind and we were no longer allowed to go on our own, so I dropped my bike on to the lawn and ran inside, my Dad was standing up in the living room, I ran up to my Dad and bear hugged him.

"Please, please, please Dad, we're 11 please let us go on our own" I begged.

My Dad laughing cuddled me and held out his hand, "You'll be needing this" he said, and he gave me some money.

"Now get gone and have fun" and with that I gave my Dad a kiss and ran back outside excitedly to Matilda.

. . .

"Quick let's go" I said and off went closing the gate behind us.

The fair was three miles away from my home, so we decided to cycle down Parrin Lane, through Monton, once we got to the Texaco petrol station we decided to take a short cut over the railway bridge, I had been this way may times before with my parents walking to Sandford so I knew the route well.

We arrived at the fair and before we knew it we had spent all of our money and it wasn't even lunchtime, so we jumped back on our bikes and headed back home. We went to Matilda's house and her mum supplied us with more money and again we set off back to the fair, for the life of me I can't recall what we were spending our money on, but yet again we were spent up, so back on our bikes and this time we headed to my house where my Dad was only too happy to give us a little more money and back we went to the fair.

We had such a great time and before long it was time to go home, so on our bikes we went and began our journey home, we took the same route as we had done back and forth all day. As we approached the railway bridge we jumped off our bikes and carried them up the steps Matilda was in front so she got back on her bike and began to cycle off, as I got to the top of the steps and was getting back on to my bike I noticed a male coming towards us, he was mid

20's very scruffy, slim build and wearing dirty jeans, he was on the opposite side of the bridge, and as I began to cycle I notice Matilda was about 10 to 15 meters ahead of me and the male was just passing her on her left, something made me feel very uneasy about this male, he was looking directly at me and had his hands down his jeans, I couldn't tell if his jeans were open or not but at eleven years of age I don't think I was exactly looking.

As I started getting closer to the male I began to speed up as I wanted to pass him as quickly as possible, he was still on the left side of the bridge and I was on the right. As I approached him, he took one of his hands out of his jeans and lunged towards me knocking me to the floor, I was entangled in my bike, the male whilst holding me down managed to move my bike as best as he could, with his torso he was pressing me into the ground, I could barely breathe due to the pressure on my chest.

I was trying with all my might to scream, but I could hardly get a word out, only small helpless sounds came out, he had one hand down his open jeans and was masturbating and with his other hands his was trying to pull my cycling shorts down, he eased the pressure on my chest, I was screaming at him to stop, telling him "No", I was screaming for my friend Matilda, screaming for anyone to come anyone to help me.

I was hitting him and trying to push him off me with one

THE TRUTH BEHIND THE UNIFORM

hand and trying to stop him from puling my cycling short down with the other, he was licking my face, trying to put his tongue in my mouth, his breath was terrible, I had never smelt anything like it, his teeth were dirty, I was violently moving my head from side to side to prevent him from putting his tongue in my mouth, he was groaning, I was hysterical, fighting for what felt like my life and then out of nowhere there was a loud noise and it startled him, he got to his knees and ejaculated over me, got to his feet and ran off towards the steps I had just climbed minutes earlier and he was gone.

I was on the floor hysterical, covered in this white fluid, I got up as quickly as I could jumped back on my bike and began to cycle as fast as my eleven year old legs could go, I wanted to get home, I wanted to feel safe, I wanted my Daddy, as I came down the bridge Matilda was there, I didn't say anything I was cycling down the alleyway as fast as my legs could take me, I came out of the alleyway and onto the main road, Monton Road, all I could think of was getting home to my Daddy, where I would feel safe.

I was cycling so fast, hysterical and looking worse for wear when two male police officers in their police van stopped at the junction noticed me, I didn't notice them, but one of the officers must have alighted the vehicle and stopped me as I was trying to cycle past, I couldn't speak through my tears but it was evident he could tell what had happened. He was asking me questions but all I could say was I wanted to go home, I wanted my Daddy. Now in all honesty I don't really recall much of what happened next but I remember being taken home in the police van. Once I was home, I remember the police officer taking my clothing, I remember calming down enough in my Daddy's presence to tell the police officers what had occurred.

My Dad and Daz were livid, I had never seen my Dad react this way to anything before, he was so angry I could see the anger in his eyes, in his actions, his gritted teeth, his clenched fists, I could see tears in his eyes and I had never seen that before, he and my uncle began to leave the house saying they were going to find this man and kill him. They were going to find the bastard and fucking kill him, I had never heard my Dad say these words before, the police officers were trying to calm my Dad and uncle but they were telling the officers in no polite way to move out of their way and let them handle it.

I screamed at my Dad and uncle to stop "please just stop" I begged them.

My Dad and Uncle Daz came back into the living room and my Dad grabbed hold of me embraced me and we cried, I couldn't stop apologising, I was apologising for making my Dad angry.

I remember my mum and siblings being present, my siblings were crying but I don't think they truly understood what had happened and my mum, well she was sat in her chair smoking a cigarette

At the age of eleven I wasn't very sexually aware, I hadn't even had a first kiss, yet I was more mature than most for my years and knew that what had occurred this fateful day, and subsequent behaviour from others would change me and affect me for years to come.

I dealt with this incident very well, I understood that there were, and are, bad people in the world and there was nothing I could have done to prevent what occurred from happening to me. Despite this, others had a different opinion. I knew Matilda had gone home and told her mum about the incident but what I didn't expect when I went around to her house a few days later was the reaction I received.

I knocked on the front to her home and Matilda answered the door, I asked her if she was coming out to play and she told me she wasn't allowed to play with me anymore, I was taken aback by this response and asked her why, she shrugged her shoulders and her mum came to the door,

"Matilda isn't allowed to play with you anymore, she doesn't play with dirty girls" she said, and with that she closed the front door.

. . .

Confused and upset I started to walk home, as I did I saw two of the boys from my class at school Stephen and Daryll, they started making fun of me saying "I liked dick" and "I liked older men wanking on me", that I was "a slag and dirty" and that their parents said "I asked for it".

I knew I was none of these yet, the words hurt, what had Matilda said? Why were they saying these hurtful things?

My emotions got the best of me, I stormed over to Stephen and Daryll, asked them to say it to my face instead of behind my back like the cowards they are, Stephen laughed and called me a slag and in a split second I pulled my arm back and punched Stephen as hard as I could in the face, he fell backwards and his nose started to bleed, Daryll started to laugh at Stephen,

"You just got decked by a girl "said Daryll

Without a moment's hesitation I served the same justice to Daryll, only it was his mouth that was bleeding, and with that I walked away laughing,

"You both just got decked by a girl and say anything about me again and I'll tell everyone" I shouted.

. . .

When I got home, I told my Dad what had happened and we laughed

"Well, those karate lessons have paid off" my Dad said.

Before long everyone I knew had heard about the sexual assault, it was in the local paper, I went Morris dancing and people were whispering about it so I was very grateful when Terry the founder and trainer of the dancing troupe came over to me and gave me a big hug and with tears in his eyes, he asked me if I was OK, he told me he had seen me on the day of the incident, he was in his car and drove past me when I was with the police officers, he turned around to see if I was ok but by the time he got back to where he saw me I had left with the police. Terry was and is such a great man and it was evident he thought the world of all the dancers and thought of us as family.

Following that incident not only had I became aware of a whole new world that a child shouldn't be aware of, but I lost a lot of people I thought were my friends. I couldn't help thinking why they would think I brought something like this upon myself? Why would adults not let their children play with me? I didn't do anything wrong and I felt like I was being punished.

WHAT'S VOLLEYBALL?

I was glad to be going to high school following the summer of 1993, most if not all of the other children from my primary school were going to a different school to me, so it was like a fresh start and one I was looking forward to.

My older sister was already at high school, she was three years older than me. It was a tougher start than I expected as my older sister wasn't a very popular girl, when I say not a very popular girl she was hated, she was bullied for being quite a promiscuous girl and unfortunately for me the girls that bullied Emily at school thought it was good idea to bully me.

They would push me into the walls, spit at me, flick cigarette ash in my hair, call me horrible names, I tolerated it for months, until one day I saw one of the girls bullying my sister between the music and maths block, spitting at her and calling her names.

It was the first time I had actually seen them behave this way towards Emily, I only knew they hated her and bullied her because they had told me when doing the same thing to me.

Emily kept telling them to stop but they continued to laugh at her, "Don't do that" I shouted as I approached them, they turned around.

"Oh, look it's the whore's sister" said one of the girls Chelsea, she was the ring leader.

"Two for one today" said another girl, she was called Jade, her trusty side kick

I presumed they meant they were going to beat us both up at the same time today, both girls really thought they were the bee's knee's, when in actual fact they were just bullies with issues of their own and found great satisfaction in feeling powerful over weaker people.

I was telling them to leave her alone, she hasn't done

anything to them when one of the girls started to flick her cigarette ash in my face.

I was standing there looking at the girls when people started to gather round, I remember thinking to myself I was going to get in trouble for the actions I was about to take.

"Is that all you've got?" I said to the ring leader Chelsea.

"Who the fuck are you talking to you scruffy bitch?" replied Jade.

Chelsea started laughing "What? you cheeky bitch!" she said.

"You heard me" I snapped back.

Chelsea wasn't happy and began calling me names, the crowds that had gathered started to shout.

"Fight! Fight! Fight!"

. . .

And with that Chelsea lunged at me and went to slap me across the face, I blocked her attack and punched her in the face, she fell into the side of the music block holding her blooded face, completely shocked, everyone around went silent, I stepped towards Chelsea and pushed her up against the wall, telling her if she came near me or my sister again and there would be more where that came from, and with that I let go and turned around, and I pointed at Jade and the rest of the bullies;

"And that goes for the rest of you too" I snapped.

From that moment on I didn't have any problems with bullies again nor did any of my siblings.

I began to enjoy school, I was making new friends though I didn't really feel like I fitted in very well, I had friends in every group but never felt like I belonged to one particular group. Even though I had made friends I began to feel a little lost at school.

Then one particular day I genuinely forgot my maths homework, I enjoyed maths and my teacher Mr Moore was surprised that I had forgotten my homework as I wasn't someone who would normally do so.

"Well Helen, you either stay in at lunchtime and write lines or you stay behind after school on Wednesday for two hours and play volleyball" Mr Moore said.

Everyone hated writing lines and I was no exception "Sorry Sir, I'll stay after school and play volleyball" I said.

"Good" replied Mr Moore.

"Excuse me Sir, but what's volleyball?" I asked.

"You'll see" he said as he walked away laughing.

True to my word that Wednesday I stayed for two hours after school and found out what volleyball was, and boy did I love it, those two hours flew by so quickly.

At the end of the session I asked Mr Moore if I could come again, he smiled and told me I could, and gave me a list of the other volleyball practice times.

From that moment I began to attend the lunch time and after school practice sessions and before I knew it, I had made the school volleyball team.

. . .

I was really good at it and Mr Moore quickly gave me the name "She-Ra" also known as the Princess of power, she was the female version of "He-Man" and a name I was quite proud to possess.

I was very athletic at school and I don't recall not being the best at any sport I took my hand to, whether that be volleyball, Badminton or track and field, yet my love for volleyball grew with every practice and I soon began to excel.

Mr Moore told me that a local team were coming in one Friday after school to take the training session with a possibility of choosing new players. I was so excited and told Mr Moore I was going to make the team. He smiled, and as he walked away said "I know".

Friday arrived and this is where I met Mark, the head coach for the local team, Manchester United, not only were they the local team but they were the best team in the country at the time.

The training session was great and though no one was officially told if they had made the team, Mr Moore and Mark pulled me aside at the end of the session and Mark told me how impressive I was. I knew then I was going to be part of the Manchester United team.

SHE'S GONE FOR GOOD

It was Friday 21st April 1995 a day that I can recall like it was only yesterday and not the 24 years it has indeed actually been. I had my usual 7pm to 9pm volleyball training for Manchester United Volleyball team. Training had finished and I left the leisure centre and headed out to my Dad's car as I always did, only this time the car was filled with all of my siblings. I found this quite odd but also quite funny as never before had they come to collect me from training.

I jumped in the back seat and noticed everyone was or had been crying. I asked my Dad what was going on and his words were;

"Your mum's left Titch".

. . .

"Pardon?" I replied.

And my Dad said those words again;

"Your mum has left".

I understood clearly what my Dad had just told me but I think I said those words out of shock and disbelief. I was confused, not because the words were confusing, I was confused with my own feelings and thoughts.

I was upset that my mum had left, but I had millions of other thoughts racing though my head about what this entailed, no more family, no more mum, no more beatings, no more fear, no more, no more, no more the list was endless.

We sat in the car outside the leisure centre for about ten minutes, yet I didn't see or hear a thing, my Dad was talking to me, but I didn't take any of it in as I was too consumed with trying to process my own thoughts.

Then I felt the warm familiar sensation I unfortunately know so well, as the tears left my eyes and started to trickle down my cheeks, I asked my Dad to take us home.

. . .

When we got home, I had composed myself, well, as much as a thirteen year old girl who's world had just fallen apart can do, I wanted to know every detail, What was she doing? What did she say? How was she?

All of these questions were answered by my Dad and he informed me my mum had been sitting in her usual chair by the window in the living room smoking a cigarette and everything was normal, then the house telephone rang around seven thirty and my mum answered it, my Dad said it was as if she was expecting the call.

My mum said a few words and laughed down the telephone then replaced the receiver and without a moment's hesitation she picked up her lighter and packet of cigarette's turned to my Dad with a smile on her face and said;

"I don't love you and I don't love the kid's, I'm leaving" and with that she walked out of the living room, took her coat off the peg in the hallway and walked out of the front door. As she walked past the window my Dad recalled her having a big smile on her face and didn't even take a moment to look through the window at the people she was leaving behind.

This wasn't enough for me, there was no reason here, I needed more answers and wanted to know why. What had we done? Why would our mum leave us? Her children? Was it true? Did she really not love us? Did she ever love us? Is that why she treated us so badly?

I had more questions than I had answers and I was confused so I can't imagine what my poor younger siblings were feeling or thinking. I wanted answers.

It was very late by the time we all went to bed that night, I think we all fell asleep through sheer emotional exhaustion.

The next morning we woke to find it wasn't a dream and mum had indeed left.

It was around 9am when I set out to find answers, I walked the three mile distance from my house to the only place I could think of my mum being, her sister Ada's house in Sandford.

Ada wasn't a nice person, whenever my mum took us round there Ada would have males round that were not much older than myself, they would be smoking, drinking alcohol and using drugs in the house and in the presence of Ada's children too.

They would store their ill-gotten gains there and along with Ada they would send us children out to steal from the shops, they would give us a back pack and we weren't to come back unless it was full. I always felt uncomfortable when I went there, but today I had a purpose.

As I approached Ada's house, I saw my mum and Ada enter the house along with some of the males I regularly saw there.

Alone, I walked up the steps and knocked on the front door, Ada opened the door.

"What do you want?" She spat.

"I want to see my mum" I replied, and Ada lied to my face and told me my mum wasn't there.

I told her I knew she was as I had just seen them all walk in to the house not five minutes earlier, at this point I remember the male I knew as "Stringer" come to the front door and tell Ada to let me in to see my mum. I walked in through the front door past Ada who called me a bitch as she pushed me into the wall. Undeterred by her cruel actions, I regained my balance and walked down the hall to the room I heard my mum's laughter coming from.

As I walked in the room, she was sat on the sofa to the left no more than a meter away from the doorway, smoking a cigarette, I stood in the doorway and there were more of the younger men I regularly saw, around the room drinking alcohol, smoking and taking drugs.

I asked my mum if we could talk and she told me we had nothing to talk about. I told her I wanted to know if she was coming back home, she started laughing at me, I asked her why she had left us and if it was true that she didn't love us.

My sheer presence had clearly angered my mum, she didn't respond to my questions until she had finished her cigarette and put it in the ashtray, as soon as she did this she leapt out of her chair and within two steps she had hold of me by the throat and pushed me up against the wall, I started to cry, the males were clearly shocked by her reaction as they jumped up, but they didn't intervene.

My mum took hold of my hair with her free hand, she let go of my throat and then began to drag me out of the room we were in and down the hallway, it felt like my scalp was going to detach from my skull. I brought both of my hands up and held on to my hair trying to release some of the tension caused by my mum's grasp, I was doing everything I could to stay on my feet and follow instead of being dragged further, I was screaming for her to let go, but all she replied was, "Shut up you little bitch".

. . .

She opened the front door and proceeded to drag me down the six or so steps, then pushed me in to the middle of the road where I fell onto the ground, she kicked me in the stomach and shouted verbal abuse at me before being pulled away by the males that were in the house but not before telling me she never loved me.

I was hysterical, curled up in pain in the middle of a normally busy road but the traffic was quiet as it was still early morning.

I then heard a familiar voice and a noticed a person crouch down to me, it was one of the older girls I had known for years Abby from the Morris dancing troupe. She helped me up off the ground and walked me to her mum's car where we got in and her mum drove me to their home where they tended to my wounds and I told them about the last 24 hours.

When I finally went home, I told my Dad what had happened and that I never wanted to see her again.

Unfortunately, that wasn't the case, my younger sisters and brother wanted to see our mum again and I didn't want them to be alone with her so arrangements were made for us to visit our mum a number of weeks later. I honestly don't know why she even wanted to see us again considering everything that had happened, but we went along to see her.

Of all places, the visit was in the Wellington Pub in Sandford. As we entered our mum was sat at a table directly opposite the entrance door. She didn't get up to greet us, so I showed my two younger sisters to the table and we all sat down. It was only me, Sarah and Amy that went, Emily didn't want to go, and Jacob was too young.

Within seconds of us sitting down a male I didn't know came to the table with two drinks and two packets of crisps and sat down next to my mum. Neither of them asked if myself or siblings wanted a drink or crisps but I didn't expect anything more.

"This is Keith my mum said".

I asked who Keith was, she laughed and kissed him then said she was going to the toilet. Whilst my mum was in the toilet my sister Amy and I started rocking on our stools, balancing our weight on the back two legs, the stools had four wooden legs and a round red velvet seat with no back. Keith told us to stop, Amy did but I didn't.

"I just told you to stop that" he snapped.

. . .

"No I replied, you're not my Dad" and then I heard my mum's voice say, "Do what he says".

"No, he isn't my Dad, I don't even know him" I replied, and as soon as I finished my sentence my mum smacked me across the face so hard it knocked me off the stool and on to the floor.

I immediately picked myself up off the floor and saw that Amy and Sarah were crying hysterically, I looked at my mum and told her she would never do that again. I took hold of my sister's hands and told them it was Okay and for them to come with me, and with that we walked out of the pub and I vowed to protect my siblings and to never see my mum again. I also promised that when I had my own children, I would be the exact opposite of her and be the best possible mummy I could be.

With mum gone things were very different around the house. There was a lot less violence that's for sure, but we had some things so ingrained in our heads it took us along time to break the habits. We no longer had to ask to do such basic things like go to the toilet, ask for food, or if we could sit on the sofa instead of the cold hard floor and these little things seemed like such a luxury.

The one thing I couldn't get used to was, the sound of my Dad crying at night, when we were all in bed, I could hear

THE TRUTH BEHIND THE UNIFORM

my Dad cry and it broke my heart knowing he felt so sad. At first I thought it was because he missed mum, but I soon realised it was because his life had been completely turned upside down and not only did he now have five children to look after, he was no longer able to work or go to the "Town Hall" pub where the local bikers met.

You don't often hear of women leaving their children with the Dad when separating, let alone back in the early 90's so I could understand my Dad's sadness.

What I couldn't understand was the change in my Dad, he began drinking more often, my Dad's friend Daz was round most evenings, and on occasions Dad was becoming aggressive too, however the most hurtful thing Dad did was tell us we were lucky he didn't put us in care because he wanted to. All of a sudden, I felt like we were a burden to him, but that said we still had some wonderful times with him.

On some weekends Dad and Daz used to put all five of us either in the back of Daz's transit van or my Dad's estate car and drive to the "Town Hall" pub. They would park down the alleyway and they would go to the pub for a few hours, but not before one of them came back with a packet of crisps and a fizzy drink for us all.

As children this was such an adventure, we had so much fun on these nights, then Dad and Daz would come back and we would all drive home. This fortunately didn't last too long, but the drinking did, when Dad would tell Daz he was going to bed which meant Daz had to leave it would cause arguments, and sometimes Daz would break something as he left, he left holes in doors and on a couple of occasions when he walked past the living room window he smashed the window.

I used to try and ask Daz to leave because I thought if I asked, he wouldn't get angry and cause fights. This worked for a while but then there were occasions when I had to get between my Dad and Daz to stop them from fighting, this mostly worked, however on a couple of occasions, I needed help.

On this one particular night, the younger children were in bed and I was in my nightdress ready for bed, it was getting late and Dad and Daz had been drinking. I said to Daz it was getting late and we all needed to go to bed but he didn't listen and continued talking with my Dad. I told him again and he said it wasn't my house, my Dad then said "well it is getting late" and before I knew it Daz was being abusive to my Dad, my Dad was trying to calm him down but it wasn't working and within minutes they were fighting. I tried to get in between them and stop them, but they continued to fight, my siblings had woken up and had come downstairs and were stood in the hall way screaming and crying, I needed help, I couldn't stop them on my own.

I don't remember why, but the home telephone was

broken and the only thing I could think of doing was running to the nearest telephone box and calling the police. I told my siblings to get upstairs and I immediately ran out of the house. It must have been past 10 o'clock as I ran down the street in my night dress and socks. It was raining and cold, but I ran as fast as I could down the street, through the pitch black alleyway and across the road to the telephone box. I was crying, not knowing what was happening at home, was my Dad ok? what about my sisters and brother?

I dialled 999 and asked for the police. I was speaking so fast, the lady on the line told me to slow down. I managed to tell the operator what was happening, she informed me some police officers were on their way to my home and to the telephone box to me. She asked me to stay talking to her and wait for the police to arrive. I told her I couldn't and I had to get home and with the reassurance that police were on their way. I put the telephone down and began to run back home as fast as I could.

I could hear the sirens in the not so far distance, and the run must have only taken a couple of minutes and as I approached the end of the alleyway that took me on to my street, the police arrived too. Before I knew it my street, garden and house was full of police officers with police vehicles everywhere, the blue flashing lights illuminating the night sky.

. . .

I was so happy to see the police officers, to know I had help and didn't have to stop them alone.

I ran to my house, a female police officer stopped me from running into the garden and asked me if I was the girl who called the police. I told her I was and that I needed to get back inside to my siblings and that the police needed to stop my Dad and Daz from fighting. She reassured me that they were no longer fighting and everyone was safe.

I was exhausted, the feeling I felt is one I now know to be of huge relief, like the world had been lifted off my young shoulders, even then I knew it wasn't a feeling a child so young should have to bear.

There were no arrests made, Daz was escorted home and once the police left, I got my younger siblings back to bed.

There was another occasion when my Dad and Daz were fighting. I can't remember the exact reason how, but my Dad's hand ended up going through a glass window on a cabinet in the living room. He instinctively recoiled his hand and within a spilt second there was blood everywhere.

I immediately ran into the kitchen and grabbed a towel and put it around my Dad's hand. Once it had absorbed some of the blood I pulled it back to see the injury, there was no skin left on the back of his hand. I could see the bones, tendons and muscle and I knew immediately we needed an ambulance. I quickly covered his hand as the bleeding was profuse. I phoned for an ambulance and my Dad was taken to hospital, he needed emergency surgery and a skin graft.

Incidents like this happened on more than one occasion, though most of the time I managed to defuse the situation before it escalated in to a situation that required police assistance. One that will always stay with me though, started as many of the others did, Daz didn't want to go home, he and my Dad began arguing and I told Daz that he shouldn't bother coming around anymore if this was how most evenings were going to end.

As he left, he shouted "Ahh shut up Titch",

"Drop Dead" I replied.

To this day I have no idea why I shouted that, I presume I was just so exhausted with the constant battles, not only that, I became anxious all the time when he was at our house, waiting for something to trigger his anger off.

The next day we received news that Daz had died, we weren't sure how it had happened, but I felt a horrible guilt, I'd told him to drop dead, had I caused this? What had happened? I had so many questions running through my head but I also felt an incredible amount of relief and then another immediate feeling of guilt for thinking such terrible thoughts.

We later found out that he asked one of his friends for some paracetamol and he gave him ecstasy pills instead, Daz took these and with the ecstasy and alcohol combination, vomited in his sleep and subsequently choked on it and died. Not too long after the same male was found murdered.

The funeral for Daz was quite something he and my Dad were or had been at some point part of a biker group, there were an incredible number of bikers who attended, and the procession of bikes that followed the hearse was quite a sight. There must have been more than a hundred motorbikes. Bikers stopped traffic to allow the whole procession to continue together.

I often felt incredibly sad that the last words I said to Daz were such terrible ones that when I later joined the police force, I went to visit Daz at the cemetery as my police training centre Sandford Park was close to where Daz was laid to rest.

PLAYING FOR ENGLAND

Volleyball became my way of forgetting everything, it was such a stress relief and a way to get away from everything at home. I began to excel, I was training at every opportunity, if I wasn't training at school or playing in school competition's, I was training and playing with the local team Manchester United and competing in tournaments. We were bringing home trophy after trophy and I loved the feeling of competing, it felt like the only time I could be free and yet focused.

Mark was also the head coach for the North England cadet's volleyball team and although I was a lot younger than the other girls, he asked me to start joining the training weekends. I was ecstatic, I couldn't wait to tell my Dad. My Dad, my nana and my granDad were so proud of me. It was an incredible feeling. I also couldn't wait to tell Mr Moore, he too was very proud of me and we had a giggle that all this started because I forgot my homework.

. . .

The first weekend I trained with the girls I was a little nervous as I had none of my team mates that were my age there, but I didn't care that I was younger than the other girls by two years plus, I knew I could keep up, I knew I was as good as, if not better than most, especially the girls that had also come from the same team as me.

I loved the weekend, I was exhausted but the feeling was amazing, I had the drive and belief I would one day be representing England in the sport I had come to love.

Before long I was asked to start training with the Manchester United senior team too which doubled my training time but I thrived playing at a higher standard. These girls were the best team in the country and I was still only 14yrs old.

Coach Mark told me some of the England cadets were chosen to go to the National trials for the England junior team and asked if I wanted to come along. I didn't need asking twice, of course I wanted to go along, I wanted to see who the best in the country were and how I compared. There were so many girls there, the atmosphere was intense, you could tell everyone there wanted to make the team.

. . .

The head coach for the England team was a man named Carl. I knew Carl as he was the head coach at Manchester United, he trained the Division one senior team.

We started with a variety of drills, so they could assess everyone's strengths and weaknesses, now my weakness was something I could do nothing about, I was only 5ft 6" tall, most of the girls towered over me, but what I lacked in height, I made up for in skill and determination. We ended the weekend mixing the teams up and playing matches against one another. I was in my element and knew I was on fire.

At the end of the weekend everyone was told if they had made the National team or not, the older girls from my local team had not made the team but I wasn't surprised considering the standard.

We were all getting ready to leave when Mark came over to me and asked to have a quiet word, Mark informed me that I had been selected to join the national team, I was so shocked and confused as I hadn't been there to try for the team because I was so much younger than everyone else, but I was so excited and ready to scream with this amazing news, but then he told me he had turned the offer down on my behalf.

I was devastated, I couldn't understand why he would do

that, I felt my heart sink and my eyes began to fill with tears, but I didn't cry, I couldn't say anything when Mark informed me that he thought I would benefit more staying with him rather than going to the national team so soon, and that the following year he would have no problem with me joining the national team.

On one hand I knew Mark was right, he was one of the best if not the best coach in the country, especially when it came to defence and defence was where I excelled. So, I took the coaches advice, even though I found it a hard pill to swallow.

At the next cadet training session everyone who didn't go to trails wanted to know who if anyone had made the team, Mark made the announcements and I remember feeling devastated that I wasn't in that small group. Mark then told the team that one more person had been selected and he told the team I had been selected too, people started to clap and some congratulate me when Mark informed them that I wouldn't be taking up the honour this year and we believed I would benefit more staying with the team.

Everyone could see the disappointment in my face, but Mark then quickly got training underway. Some of the girls from my local team started to be different with me, they had not been selected yet thought they were so much better than me. I knew it was jealousy and I didn't let it affect me.

The following year I was once again selected to join the England Team, and nothing was going to stop me this time.

The feeling of your countries National anthem being played in your honour is one I will never forget. A huge sense of pride from knowing that you are the best in the country. I loved the feeling playing for England gave me, however once again there was a class difference within the team, most of the girls were from the South and came from affluent backgrounds.

I was the only one who was from a poor background and needed financial help in order to participate in the training. Volleyball in this country doesn't get much funding despite it being the number one sport for females around the world. The good thing was, the manager and coaches valued my talent so much they were the ones who arranged for my sponsorship and grants. My Dad had four other children to take care of so he helped when he could, and I could feel his sense of pride.

We were having training camps up and down the country, we got to travel to so many different countries for international tournaments. Countries I only ever dreamed of visiting. We had European championships in Turkey, where we were the first English team to ever take a set off another team and from tournament statistics, I was the best player in my position and third best defender at the tournament, that was a huge achievement for a girl from a council estate in Salford.

Unfortunately, at eighteen years old I was once again subjected to a sexual assault, I was on a train sat by myself for a short while, I was sat next to the window, the train was relatively empty when an older male came and sat next to me. I didn't think anything of it and was keeping myself to myself, when suddenly I felt a hand on my left leg, I froze, I held my breath for a few seconds trying to take in what was happening.

A million thoughts were racing through my head, the male had placed his bag on his lap, whether this was to hide his erection or to cover up what he was doing I don't know, however he continued caressing my leg with his right hand, moving higher and higher until he reached my groin area.

I grabbed his hand turned to him and told him to get the fuck off me followed by a barrage of expletives, he jumped up from his seat and began to walk down the aisle. I then burst out crying, I couldn't believe this could happen to me again, what was so wrong with me? Passengers alerted the conductor and the police were called, luckily we'd told the conductor before the train stopped at Birmingham New Street, the next train station, they therefore kept everyone on the train.

I spoke with police, gave them a detailed description and

they searched the train for the male. As I was still in my seat they brought the same male back to me for identification purposes, I confirmed it was the same male however he had tried to disguise himself and changed not only clothes but his facial accessories and hair too. Clearly he knew what he was doing. We went to court, the solicitor was just as bad as the pervert who assaulted me, trying to make out I was lying and seeking attention, it turned out it wasn't the first time this pervert had been arrested for sexual offences, he was found guilty and sentenced to time in prison. I couldn't thank the police officers enough, they were extremely professional and incredibly supportive throughout the whole process.

When you think over 90% of sexual assaults are committed by a perpetrator the victim knows, you can see how unlucky I was to be sexually assaulted on two separate occasions by complete strangers.

With college behind me and a BTEC in Sports science under my belt I was heading to the top sporting university in the country. I would be there with the majority of the other girls from the National squad and we would train regularly.

I was excited by the opportunity but also conflicted as to whether I should go or not. My Dad was unable to work due to my three younger siblings who were all still under sixteen years and my brother had been diagnosed with

ADHD along with other behavioural issues and was regularly sent home from school. I was in two minds if I should go to university or stay home and get a job so I could help out financially and with my family.

I struggled with the decision for weeks as I knew I needed a degree to continue and become a primary school teacher or physical education teacher, I had some wonderful teachers and still believe to this day that teachers are fundamental in helping build our children's foundations in many aspects of life, especially when some children don't have the stability at home, some teachers are integral role models for those children.

I also believe that sport plays a huge role in teaching children and young people many of the disciplines needed and valued in life. I had always considered becoming a police officer too. I never forgot how safe the police officers made me feel when I was younger. I wanted to protect children from being victims of domestic and sexual abuse too. I knew I had a lot to offer not only from an empathic perspective, but from a first hand experience perspective too, I could relate to some of the people I would be helping. I made decision, I wasn't going to university, I would stay home and get a job until I could join the police force, that way I could also help my Dad out financially. I applied to the police force as soon a I was age eligible.

I continued to play volleyball for both Manchester United

and by this time the England senior team, though I found the senior team to be very bitchy and clicky and god help you if you were a threat to one of their positions. I found it hard to gel with the girls, they were very superficial and most of them had come from privileged back grounds and had their heads in the clouds about life, I was a council estate girl from a poor background, I had experienced the negative side of life and knew the realities of the big wide world, I had no tolerance for idle chit chat and the latest celebrity gossip.

THE POLICE FORCE

I was flying through the process of becoming a police officer, all the tests were spread out over a number of months and held at either Sandford Police Headquarters or Sandford Park police training school. It was a long process, I passed the Maths and English exams, the observation tests and group discussions tests too.

Then it was the fitness test which is where a lot of people fail, it consisted of the bleep test to level 8.2, a speed and agility test, running around cones and jumping over small apparatus in a set amount of time, the grip test and the push pull test. I sailed through the fitness and got through to the final interview.

On the day of the interview I was incredibly nervous, I entered the room and I was greeted by three people all of senior rank within the force and one from human resources. I thought I answered the questions well and felt confident as I left the room.

The five minute wait outside was tense and felt a lot longer when the door opened and I was welcomed back into the room. I sat down and I was told I answered the questions well, hearing this I was sure I was going to be congratulated so I was extremely disappointed when the follow up was:

"We don't think you have enough life experience to become a police officer as yet, maybe in six to twelve months time reapply and come back".

In my head I was shouting "Are you serious!!!". I probably have more life experience in my twenty years than you three sat there put together. But I kept myself together and thanked them for their time. I walked back to my Dad who was waiting for me in the car and as soon as I shut the door, I couldn't stop myself from crying, I was so disappointed.

I wanted to reapply straight away, but I had to wait for the mandatory six month period to lapse before I could. When I did reapply I had to go through the whole process again, yet this time the fitness test wasn't anywhere near as bad, not that it was challenging the first time but they had reduced the bleep test pass level to just above level 5 and we no longer had to do the push pull test or the speed and agility test, so the fitness test was a breeze. I had made it to the final interview, I wasn't going to fail this time.

They asked me to enter the room and I was even more nervous than the first time. Then as I sat down they introduced themselves, they weren't the same people as last time but once again it was senior ranking officers, they were more friendly and less intimidating. They told me to relax and offered me a glass of water and as I reached for it I accidentally knocked it over, it spilt all over the table and it was fast approaching their paperwork.

"Oh shit, sorry sugar I meant" I said whilst feeling my face burn from the embarrassment.

"I'm so sorry" I said.

To my relief they started to laugh, they told me not worry about the water, the slip up or the interview and we wiped the spillage up. As we sat down one of the officers asked me where I had travelled from and how long it had taken me to get here today, and for a couple of minutes it was general chit chat, he told me a little about himself too. I didn't realise at the time, but he was doing this to help me relax and it worked, without me really noticing they started to ask the interview questions and before I knew it the interview was over.

. . .

"See it wasn't that bad was it" one of the officers said as I blushed and laughed replying that it wasn't, they asked me to leave the room for a moment and they would call me back in shortly. As I left my heart sank, I'd just blown my opportunity, they wouldn't want a clutz in the police force.

As I left, I envisioned them saying they wouldn't trust me with a pen let alone a baton or someone's life. I took a seat in the waiting area and was greeted by another willing victim heading for his interview, he smiled and asked me how it went, I shook my head and said disaster, as the door opened and they asked me to return to the room, this can't be good, I had only just left the room two minutes ago.

"Helen, please take a seat" said one of the officers.

"Thank you" I said as I sat down.

"So how do you think that went?" said the same officer.

I let out a nervous laugh "It could have gone better" I replied.

He then informed me that I had given great answers to all of the questions and exhibited great knowledge and common sense on how to handle various situations and I would be an asset to the police force.

"Really?" I replied.

"Yes, congratulations Helen you have passed the interview" he replied.

They then told me I had to head to the force Doctors to have my medical assessment and pending the outcome of the medical, I would be joining Sandford police force.

I was so excited and couldn't thank them enough, I felt like I was walking on air as I left the interview room.

I arrived at the location for my medical and was congratulated by the doctor, my medical went without a problem and the doctor asked me to confirm an answer on my application.

"It says on here you don't consume alcohol Helen" he said.

"Yes, that's correct" I replied thinking I'm not lying honestly.

. . .

When the doctor laughed and said "This job will change that".

Well, "Thanks for the warning Doc" I replied, and we began laughing.

"Well, Helen, congratulations you have passed the medical assessment" the Doctor informed be afterwards.

I couldn't wait to get to the car to tell my Dad who had been waiting for me. I walked out of training centre as fast as my legs could take me as I got passed security I could see my Dad in the car and I practically ran to him. Goodness knows what I looked like, as I got to the car my Dad was fast asleep, we had been there for over three hours. I opened the door and shouted "I passed" and my Dad woke from his deep slumber,

"Ay, what?" was his sleepy reply and I laughed and told him I'd passed, and he hugged me. He was so happy for me.

A few weeks later I received a confirmation letter with a December 2003 start date, with instructions to go for a uniform fitting.

It was only April so I had plenty of time before starting my new career, my boyfriend Simon and I decided to go on a holiday to America in the August before I started, three weeks travelling the West coast, I couldn't wait. I then received a telephone call in June from the police recruitment informing me they wanted me on a July intake date instead of December, I told them of my pending 'paid for' holiday but they advised me that if I didn't take the date, I wouldn't be accepted so I obviously agreed to the new start date.

Luckily my boyfriend at the time was very understanding and thankfully we only lost our deposit for the holiday.

This was my first experience of it's the police's way or the highway.

The new start date meant I had to get my uniform fitting in sooner than expected. I attended Sandford Bank, another police training site where I was measured for all my uniform and then I had to try it on. I was stood there looking at my reflection in the mirror, I couldn't believe I finally had my police uniform on, I looked like a real police officer and couldn't stop smiling. I left Sandford Bank with bags of police kit, when I got home I couldn't help but do a fashion show for my Dad and siblings. Dad was so proud, as was I.

Monday, July 21st 2003, I headed to Sandford Park, our

police training centre in Sandford, to begin my training. This was my first day wearing my police uniform as an actual police officer and not just in front of the mirror. I was nervous yet excited, I arrived at Sandford Park and went to my class room, where we were met by police officer Lisa who was to be out training officer, Lisa was a lovely lady and made everyone feel relaxed.

The first two weeks with Lisa were to get us learning some basics before our attestation ceremony, all new police officers are required to swear an oath to uphold the law before a magistrate and a senior police officer. Once we have made this oath, we are officially sworn in as police officers and only then can we execute police powers.

The text of the oath;

"I….. of …. do solemnly and sincerely declare and affirm that I will well and truly serve the Queen in the office of Constable, with fairness, integrity, diligence and impartiality, upholding fundamental human rights and according to equal respect to all people, and that I will, to the best of my power, cause the peace to be kept and preserved and prevent all offences against people and property, and that while I continue to hold the said office I will to the best of my skill and knowledge discharge all the duties thereof faithfully according to the law".

. . .

For the ceremony we had to wear our formal/ceremonial uniform or "Number one's" as they were called, and we were allowed to have family members present. The ceremony was held in the evening and I was happy to have my Dad, my nana and my sister Amy present, following the ceremony we were allowed to take photographs and it was a very proud moment for everyone.

Once the first two weeks at Sandford park were complete we then had a 12 week residential from mid August to the end of October at our police training school in Sandford. There were officers from many other forces there too.

It was here we felt some hate for the police for the first time. A documentary called the secret policeman had aired during our residential on BBC exposing racism within Sandford Police. It was a journalist who went through the recruitment process and became a police officer and therefore an undercover reporter to expose the racism in the force.

It was a disgrace and I was ashamed to be part of a force that had this behaviour within it, the force publicly said it was also disgusted with this behaviour and wasn't something they tolerate, though with what I know now I think it was only embarrassed at it being made public.

Due to this documentary being aired, we were receiving

verbal abuse when we left the campus, some of the officers vehicles were being damaged at the training centre, people wanted to cause trouble and tried to entice some of my fellow colleagues to engage in fights, when collected by taxi drivers from the training centres they told us we were free to put our pillowcases on our heads and be the KKK, things were that bad we were advised not to leave the centre unless it was a necessity until things had calmed down.

Despite what I saw in the documentary, for me, being a police officer was an honour, and wearing the uniform was a real privilege, to know that you are in a position to help someone when they need it most or at the most difficult time of their lives, help them feel safe and secure was something I felt blessed to do, however the reality of the police was much different.

I was assigned to A block in Sandford and my first day with my team was December 10th, 2003, it was a 07:00am day shift. I was incredibly nervous as this wasn't training anymore.

I reported to the parade room where I met my team and had my first briefing. My first two sergeants were Matt Carp who was a very sweet softly spoken man and to this day still reminds me of the boxer Chris Eubank and Fred Mitchell who was also a kind and funny man, though I didn't think so on my first day when he threw me in at the deep end and asked me to introduce myself to the team and tell them a little bit about myself, I was so nervous, I felt me face go bright red and my cheeks start to burn, I don't even recall what I said after my name.

After the briefing Sergeant Carp assigned duties and informed me my first tutor would be PC Simon Hart. Oh, great I thought, this is the guy I just sat and listened to explaining how he had just been allowed to drive police vehicles again after being suspended for knocking an old man over who was crossing the road, whilst on a "blue light" run and all he did was take the piss out of everyone whilst looking like the moodiest guy you could ever meet.

Parade was over, everyone left the room and went into the officers writing room. I must have looked like a nervous puppy, waiting for a command, no one was in any rush to get out and about and everyone sat around either chatting, doing paperwork or on the computers.

"Charlie you've been relieved of brew bitch now we have a new proby, show her the ropes shouted a voice from across the room. I later found out he was called Stan, his father was one of our superintendents.

Charlie started laughing as did everyone else, I'd heard about this, when the new probationary officer or 'proby' joined the team they would be the one who makes the whole teams tea and coffee at the start of parade and any other time it was demanded really, you couldn't say no, if you did, well let's just say it's not worth saying no, it was a tradition and an initiation.

Charlie came over to me and we started talking he showed me where the teams brew kit was, it actually had its own little locker, there are a few things cops are renowned for stealing, brew kit, food, uniform and pens I kid you not, we're all guilty of at least one of them, intentionally or not.

Charlie was five weeks ahead of me, so it was nice to know I wasn't the only new kid on the block, he was lovely, a really sweet guy. As we were walking back, Simon my tutor walked out of the writing room.

"Come on" he said, he didn't look impressed to have this new puppy to look after.

I nervously followed him to the vehicle, he double checked I had everything and told me we were going to have a little tour of the division, great I thought at least I wasn't being thrown in at the deep end and with that thought we drove out of Sandford North Police station.

We had not been out of the police station 30 seconds when we stopped at a set of traffic lights and Simon asked me if I had a HORT1 pad, this is a ticket to request the driver of a vehicle to produce their driving documents at a police station within seven days of receiving one.

"Yes" I replied nervously.

"Good, you'll need it" he said laughing.

And with that he pointed to a guy who was driving his vehicle whilst combing his hair and using an electric razor and nearly bumped into the vehicle in front of him.

Simon turned the police car around to follow the vehicle and as we pulled up behind it, he switched on the emergency equipment used to alert a driver you wanted them to pull over, the klaxons and blue lights came on and the driver immediately pulled over right outside the police station we had just left.

I was incredibly nervous, and Simon couldn't stop laughing at me and I had one thought running through my mind:

"Shit, Shit, Shit, what do I do? Do I need to say the caution, what is the caution? crap, crap, crap".

"I thought you were going to ease me in gently" I said.

. . .

Laughing Simon replied, "Nope, get out".

And with that we both got out of the vehicle and to my surprise when my knees stopped knocking and my hands stopped shaking, I issued my first HORT1 and dealt with my first incident as a real police officer. Issuing the form was a small task yet I felt incredibly proud of myself. As a police officer you deal with hundreds of incidents and make hundreds of arrests yet you always remember your firsts, your first ticket or first arrest.

After only a few days it seemed my team didn't trust me, apparently, I was too posh and too well spoken to be a police officer and suspicions arose that I was a journalist. My nickname quickly became ITV or BBC, I tried to laugh it off, but they insisted on checking my body armour and other uniform items for microphones and hidden cameras at the start of shifts, my food and other items were marked BBC or ITV too, this was all because of the sleeping police man documentary that had aired on ITV recently, I was mortified but tried not to show it.

As the shifts and checks of my uniform continued to my relief they began to relax and realise I was just another proby with no underhand intentions and I was invited to the teams Christmas night out in Manchester, I remember getting a warning from Jan, one of my other female colleagues, she told me she no longer went on works social events as they always ended up with some kind of trouble. We were a bunch of police officers, law abiding people, I mean how bad could the trouble be.

We met early in Manchester, and everyone was having a great time. Following the meal, we moved to another livelier venue, it was here I started to realise what Jane meant. We were all having a great time laughing and joking until Nick one of my colleagues said to the group.

"I bet someone ten pounds to go and take that Paki's turban"

I was mortified, I couldn't believe what I had just heard, the group starting laughing and bids were quickly rising. Not only could I not believe the derogatory terminology that was being used by my team, a team of police officers, I couldn't believe they were so uneducated not to know this man was Sikh.

They were calling this man a "Fucking Paki" and a "Rag head" I was so embarrassed. I told them to stop but they ignored me and continued with the bidding and name calling, the bidding reached £250 when one of the team agreed to do it. I didn't know what to do, I was disgusted, I had just joined my team, I turned around and saw Matt our sergeant stood at the bar talking to someone, he was completely oblivious to what was currently going on. I walked over to Matt and told him what was about to happen, he couldn't believe what he was hearing, he marched right over to the team and told them to get out of the pub.

We all left the pub and Matt told us he would deal with us when we were next on duty and with that he left. The group burst out laughing.

We decided to move on to another pub. Charlie came over to me and asked what had happened as we were going to the next pub.

Despite what had just happened everyone was still in a jovial mood. As we were stood talking in the next pub the team were taking bets on who could drink a pint of top shelf spirits that had just been ordered. I was stood talking to Phil, an older male on the team, he was heavily intoxicated, as we were talking Peter pulled his trousers and boxers down and stood holding his erect penis.

"What are you doing Peter? Pull your trousers up" I said,

"Does that make you moist" he said whilst rubbing his erect penis, "Is your pussy nice and wet? You want this don't you" he continued.

I was disgusted, this man was an experienced police officer and I couldn't believe he was behaving this way.

"You are disgusting, pull your trousers up" I said,

He ignored me and continued to rub his erect penis whilst saying "You want this don't you? Tell me your pussy is wet".

Just as Peter said that, my tutor Simon saw what Peter was doing and came storming over, Simon was furious and told Peter to pull his trousers up, some of the other team members were shouting and hollering finding the whole thing funny.

Peter pulled his trousers up and walked away calling me a spoil sport, I stood there looking at Simon, thinking what the fuck just happened. He asked me if I was Okay, I couldn't believe what some of these people were like, but they weren't just people they were police officers too, and they arrest people for the same things I had witnessed from this evening.

I told him I was going home and he waited with me whilst I got a taxi.

Whilst waiting for the taxi a few of the team came out

asking why I was leaving, I was told if I wanted to get on with the team, I shouldn't say anything to anyone.

I left in my taxi, I was still in shock about what had just happened and now I had the dilemma of reporting Peter for his behaviour and becoming an outcast on the team or staying quiet. They already thought I was a journalist of some sort and had treated me as an outcast and just as I got them to believe me, this happens. I wanted to be accepted by the team, these are the people I need to rely on if my life was in danger and I needed back up. What do I do?

I was dreading the next shift we gathered for parade and no one mentioned anything about what happened the night before, it was like it had never happened.

The Sergeants came in to parade and true to his word sergeant Carp gave the team a right bollocking, he was furious and rightly so, I was sat praying he wouldn't tell them it was me that told him, it was the last thing I needed right now, to be known as a grass.

POLICE RACISM

I was flying through my first few months and aside from the initial problems I was getting on well with my team. I was meeting the criteria in my personal development portfolio and enjoying being a police officer.

After a few months Sergeant Carp and Sergeant Mitchell were moved to other posts and we had the misfortune of two new sergeants. A female Sergeant Rita Wall and Sergeant Rob Turner.

Sergeant Wall was assigned as my team sergeant, this meant she would be the one to evaluate my progression and development as a probationary police officer and if I was fit to be confirmed in rank. I got the distinct impression she didn't like me.

. . .

When new sergeants or inspectors come to the team, they always like to run things their own way and make a stamp on the team, these two sergeants were no exception.

They decided to shake things up and change who everyone was partnered with, no one liked that. I was now partnered with a guy name Rich Hulme, he was someone who like to joke around, elaborate and embellish things quite a lot, he had previous military experience and enjoyed sharing his stories. He was a very hyper guy, always bouncing around like a child with too much sugar. We were assigned Rich's regular beat "A Beat "which was Old Sandford.

The demographic of Old Sandford consisted predominantly of Black and Asian residents. It also happened to be afflicted by high incidents of gang related crime and bordered a notorious gang area. It was the first time I had been on patrol alone with Rich.

Rich became my regular partner. He was lazy and hard work, he thought because he had a probationer with him, he didn't have to do any work, because I would do it all. He made various comments about me being his "Proby bitch" and he only had to drive us from incident to incident barking orders, smoking in the police vehicle and stopping at his parent's home for regular breaks whilst I waited in the car.

. . .

With this behaviour it was clear Rich was becoming more relaxed around me as he started to say little off the cuff remarks and making comments about various people we encountered.

On one particular shift, Rich and I were once again patrolling Old Sandford when he was ranting about a victim of crime we had just assisted.

On previous shifts Rich had mentioned ideal sniper spots around Old Sandford but had never elaborated further. He had a fascination with firearms, I presumed this was because of his military back ground. He would often make various firearm gestures with his hands and arms and pretend to "Pop" people, making comments like, "as a sniper you could pop people good from here", nothing that caused me any concern. However, on this particular shift Rich pointed out his favourite spot he would use as a sniper. I never imagined the comments that would come next.

We were on our way to our next incident in Old Sandford, we were stationary at a set of traffic lights, Rich raised his arms to make a sniper rifle action, one arm outstretched and one in towards his face as the trigger hand and closing one eye as if to focus on his target. This was a normal Rich action, however, on this occasion Rich began to say

. . .

"Pop, pop, pop the monkeys, I'd pop the little Niggars one by one".

"What the fuck Rich?" I said "You can't say shit like that".

"Don't tell me you're a Nigger lover".

"You make me sick Rich" I said.

He started laughing and tried to pretend he was joking but I had heard enough and told him so. He was a disgrace, a disgrace as a man and a disgrace as a police officer. We had a heated argument.

We arrived at the next location, it made me sick to enter this person's house knowing what Rich would be thinking about them. I dealt with the incident and we left.

There was silence in the car on the way back to the station, I was livid as we got out Rich called my name, I turned around;

"Are we Okay?" He said.

. . .

"We are far from Okay; you are a racist piece of shit" I said as I turned and walked away.

I went in the writing room to complete the paperwork for the end of shift. I had no choice but to speak with my sergeant about this, not only did I not want to be partnered with such a racist person, but I believed he should not hold the position of police officer.

I went to speak with my sergeant, I informed her of what had happened and maybe in my naivety I expected her to understand and take matters further. However, she told me I wasn't a team player and there had been numerous complaints about me not being a team player. She told me should would deal with it and I should go home.

It was never spoken about again. Seems it was one of many things that the police hide under the carpet.

Rich and I were never partnered together again, and I was very thankful of that, though I couldn't help but wonder if anything had been actioned in relation to what I reported.

On Friday and Saturday evenings as a team, we would all get together in the people carrier or "Fun bus" as it was affectionately known. This was so we could patrol and keep an eye on the local pubs and clubs and be called to any public disorders that occurred.

On this particular night we were all in the fun bus, there must have been eight of us, when we were driving down Sandford Road, as we were driving past one of the pubs, I noticed a fight taking place between three males, I told Leon our driver to stop and we got out of the van. We were on the opposite side of the road to the pub, so we had to run across the road, there were now a few people standing watching the fight.

As I approached the three males fighting, I grabbed hold of one male and began to pull him away from the fight, as I was doing this I noticed a baton coming towards my face, luckily, I moved my head in time and the baton missed by millimetres. I saw it was Rich.

"Fucking hell Rich" I shouted.

As I shouted this, I noticed Rich had placed the baton around the male's throat.

My male had calmed down at this point, so I arrested and handcuffed him, a colleague who came to assist me took my prisoner to the van for transporting.

. . .

As I turned around, I could see the situation had calmed down, another colleague had arrested another male from the fight, however I noticed Rich had his male face down on the floor, Rich still had his baton around the male's throat, pulling his head up with his knee pushed in the middle of the males back pushing him into the ground. The male was clearly struggling to breathe yet Rich continued to be verbally abusive to the male. I could see the aggression in Rich's face.

"Rich get off him" I shouted, Rich released his baton and our colleague Leon came over and got the male up off the floor and walked him across to another van that had arrived for transporting the prisoners to the police station.

We didn't have chance to discuss what had just happened as the prisoners needed to be taken to the police station and witness details obtained.

When we arrived at the police station, I booked my prisoner into custody.

Leon then brought the male in that Rich had used his baton on. One of the first questions the custody Sergeants asks when booking a prisoner in to the custody suite is who is the arresting officer.

. . .

Leon and I said Rich, Rich was in the custody suite and the sergeant told Rich to come and book his prisoner in. I couldn't believe what came out of Rich's mouth.

"It's not my prisoner Sarge, I haven't arrested him"

"What?" the custody sergeant said.

"I haven't arrested him Sarge" Rich repeated

"Then who has?" said the custody sergeant.

I couldn't believe my ears, Rich had not only used excessive force to detain this male, but he hadn't actually arrested him either.

Leon arrested and cautioned the male and proceeded to book him into custody.

We couldn't believe what had happened that night, I spoke up and said I was going to speak to the Sergeant about what had happened when Leon said as senior officer on the team, he would report the incident to the sergeant.

. . .

The next day Leon reported what had happened to the sergeant, and it was taken further. We were all asked to provide a statement for the internal affairs to investigate. At a later date we were all interviewed by internal affairs.

We were never informed of the outcome; we rarely are with those kinds of proceedings. However, you think following his actions on that night he would receive some kind of punishment, that didn't seem the case. Rich was transferred to the force priority robbery unit, this is a sought after unit where many officers apply to become a part of, so it didn't seem a punishment at all, in fact the next time I saw Rich, he said he was having a great time and loved it. There was more over time and it was much better than being on the team as a response officer.

This was just the start of me realising there are too many bad apples within the police force.

We were called to a party that had overflowed on to the streets, there were people fighting everywhere, it was so bad we had to request back up from the patrols on the south of the division, there were easily 20 plus people in various groups fighting. There were police officers everywhere trying to defuse the different situations, people were being arrested left right and centre.

. . .

As I was arresting a male he became violent towards me causing numerous injuries including a fractured tooth, it was clear I needed assistance, a couple of colleagues came to assist and as we were trying to get him into the cage in the rear of the police van he kicked me about the torso, and with his handcuffs on brought his hands down on top of a colleagues head splitting it open. When we finally got the situation under control it was evident there were far too few officers to handle the situation, it was by definition a riot but you will very rarely get the police, council or government to say or define it as such because they view this as a loss of control by the police.

Following this incident, we were asked to complete a form about what happened in regard to this situation, what was the cause, how we could have improved. I was as honest as I always will be on the form and wrote we had insufficient resources and this caused the incident to get out of hand, we lost control for a moment and if we had more officers the incident would have been diffused sooner with less persons and officers being injured and with that, I submitted my response.

A few days later I was partnered with one of the older female team members. She wasn't a particularly nice woman or police officer for that matter, but she was a yes sir no sir type. We were requested to attend an incident so we went to our vehicle parked in the station car park. Once inside the car she said,

. . .

"I heard what you wrote on your report about the incident the other night".

"Who told you what I wrote?" I asked,

"It doesn't matter who told me, what matters is you need to change what you wrote" she snapped.

"I won't be doing that, that was the whole reason we lost control of the incident" I said,

"People don't need to know we lost control of an incident, what's it going to achieve?" she snapped.

"It's not about what it's going to achieve as they will probably do nothing, but at least I know I informed them of the real reasons why, I'm not going to kiss arses to get far in this job and I'm not a yes sir no sir girl", I said angrily,

"You're not making any friends here Helen and you won't get far in the police when you challenge them like that. You are causing problems for yourself" she replied.

"I wondered why they partnered us together today, now I

know, you don't intimidate me, and I won't change my report, I stand by what I said", I replied.

We didn't say anything more and we were never partnered together again.

A few days later a friend of mine, Sally Hall, who was also a police officer at the same station, was arrested for possessing, supplying and offering to supply a class A drug, namely cocaine, at her home address after a night out. One of Sally's friends reported her to the police for the offences, alleging Sally kept the cocaine in her kitchen cupboards and on the night in question took the cocaine from the kitchen cupboard, and using a nightclub card cut the drugs up into five lines, snorted one herself and offered the others to her friends, to which some obliged. Sally denied the allegations profusely, stating the person who reported her was making false accusations because Sally wanted to change the stables where she kept her horse, and this displeased the accusers.

Having spent many a night out with, and over at Sally's house I had no reason not to believe her story, I had never witnessed any drugs at Sally's house nor in her possession on the many nights out we had. However, my doubts began to creep in when evidence came to light, not only were traces of cocaine found in hair samples the police had taken from Sally, but traces of cocaine were also found on a nightclub card found at Sally's house, though it was in a different name, it matched the story of the accuser. For those that are unaware, cocaine does not leave its marks at the root of the hair, but to specific areas and is there until the strands of hair fall out or is cut off above the cocaine marks.

Sally asked myself and a mutual colleague friend to be character witnesses at her trail, however we were advised not to by senior supervision, we therefore declined to do so.

After a twelve day trial, Sally was found not guilty of all offences much to her relief, she was still suspended pending an internal investigation. However, a few weeks after the trail Sally confessed to me that it was in actual fact true, needless to say I haven't spoken to Sally since and do not know if she is still a serving police officer and remains with the police force.

It wasn't long after this one Saturday afternoon, I drove to work and noticed almost all of the police vehicles were in the police yard, this was highly unusual and meant none or few officers were out on patrol, I parked my vehicle and went into the police station expecting to be met by any of the officers on the shift before me, but this wasn't the case, the police station was dead, it was like a ghost town, the only other officers around were from my team and they were all wondering the same thing, where was everyone?

We then had our briefing and we were informed that the

whole team on the shift before us were being spoken to, arrests had been made and an investigation was underway, they were on a team night out the previous evening and five members of the team were caught snorting cocaine in the toilets of a nightclub.

MY PRIDE, HER PREJUDICE

My relationship with my sergeant was becoming very tough indeed. Everything I did was being dissected and scrutinised, I couldn't do anything right.

I'm not the best police officer in the world but I knew I was a good one, I was learning and making mistakes along the way which any probationary police officer would. However, I was constantly in my sergeant's office, being told I was incompetent and doing things wrong. She wasn't allowing me to make positive progression with my personal development portfolio and making negative comments all of the time. I was rapidly losing my confidence.

I was told if this continued, she wouldn't advise I was competent enough to be confirmed in rank and she would have my probationary period extended. I was so deflated. I found myself agreeing to everything that was said to make life easier and to try and get through my probation. Before I knew it, I was carrying so much work I felt I was drowning in crimes and enquiries and making basic mistakes. I felt this sergeant was using me for her own personal development, she needed to have a "problem officer" to progress in her development and I felt I was made to be hers. I couldn't help but think was this because I'd made the complaint about my racist colleague.

I had one incident where we attended a house as a concern for welfare, called in by the ambulance service, the person in question was suffering with mental health issues and was trying to end their life by cutting themselves with pieces of glass, as we approached to try prevent her from doing further harm to herself she would try to attack us with the glass.

The first thing the guys wanted to do was use their CS spray and physically take her to the ground to disarm her, but it was clear from what she was saying she was struggling with something and didn't think we would understand.

I asked them to give me a minute with her and let me talk to her, I asked her what wouldn't we understand. I asked her to talk to me and I would listen and how could we understand if she didn't allow me the opportunity to listen. I think it was one of the first times she had ever been treated with respect by the police and asked how we could help instead of physically man handling her so no force would be used to restrain her, it was the first time someone was willing to listen.

Slowly she began to calm down and share her story with me, I listened to her empty her soul. She was so broken and traumatised, she didn't think someone like myself would understand her pain. When she finished, she was calmer and more at ease with me. I wanted her to know she was not alone, so I took it upon myself to take the glass from her, hold her hand and sit with her on the sofa, I shared with her a demon of my own, my own story of a sexual assault when I too was a child. She broke down crying and gave me a hug followed by "you do understand".

Sometimes all somebody wants is someone to listen, someone to understand and to know they are not alone.

I managed to get her to go to the hospital with the ambulance crew and I attended with her, I wanted her to know she wasn't alone, to show her she could get help and that she is worth living.

I didn't realise Sergeant Wall had turned up at the house whilst I was talking with the female and followed the ambulance to the hospital.

. . .

Once I left the female in the care of the hospital, I was going back to the police station with Sergeant Wall. I was so proud of myself, this was the reason I joined the police force, so I was extremely disheartened when Sergeant Wall told me I was unprofessional for sharing my story with the lady, it showed why I wasn't ready to be confirmed in rank and she was going to recommend an extension to my probationary period.

Weeks passed by and nothing was getting any easier, I was told my probation was going to be extended and I was devastated, I didn't believe I deserved that.

I ended up with an injury to my shoulder, I informed my sergeant of the injury and that I didn't want to be off work sick. I had taken Doctors advice and they said I could work but not wear my body armour and would have to be office based for a short time.

After a couple of days Sergeant Wall came in to the office and told me there was a young offender down in the cells that had been arrested and she wanted me to deal with him.

I informed her again I wouldn't be able to do it as I was in pain with my shoulder and unable to wear my body armour, I wouldn't be able to protect myself should anything happen.

. . .

"You want to get through your probation don't you" she replied whilst handing me the paperwork, the officers will be in to update you.

Of course, I wanted to get through my probation, she was already making it extremely difficult for me, so I dared not give her another reason to try and fail me.

It was a simple enough case of the offender had been caught with drugs in his possession. As the prisoner was a juvenile, he needed an appropriate adult. A short while later his appropriate adult arrived.

I went to the front desk to collect the appropriate adult. As with all visitors they have to come into the police station via a secure door from the reception area. I opened the door and went to speak with the appropriate adult who was a relative of the offender.

I could immediately tell he was heavily intoxicated and therefore unable to act as a responsible appropriate adult. I was explaining this to him when he became verbally abusive and violent towards me pinning me up against the wall. My back had hit the wall quite hard and I was in a lot of pain, luckily, I had put my radio in my pocket and managed to call for assistance. I broke free of the male and managed to arrest and detain him against the wall until assistance arrived, I was so happy to see one of the biggest officers in the station come running through the door. Taking the male from me and placing him in handcuffs and promptly taking him to join his relative in the cells.

I was in so much pain, I was struggling to walk. One of my colleagues could see this and took me to a side office to make me a cup of tea.

Sergeant Wall came into the office to ask what had happened, I informed her of the circumstances, I gave her all of the information for her to complete the relevant injury on duty forms, I just wanted to go home because I was in so much pain, however Sergeant Wall made me complete any paperwork needed before I went home despite my visible pain.

The next few days I was in agony I could barely walk, so needed time off work and called in sick.

I told them it was an injury on duty, and I was off work for around nine months, following an MRI scan it seemed I had sustained a bulged disc from the incident, and it was causing an immense amount of pain.

During this time, I had a couple of "Welfare" visits from Sergeant Sift and Inspector Branch, I had only encountered Sergeant Sift on a couple of occasions previously and I didn't particularly like the man. He was a lad's lad, one of the guys and seemed he didn't particularly have time for women.

On one occasion when they came around, Sergeant Sift took it upon himself to look through my belongings and pick up my medication which were on my dining room table and ask me if these were what I was taking for the injury, I said yes, they were and he then continued to ask me how many a day was I taking. I told him that was between myself and my Doctor. It seemed these checks were more of an interrogation than a welfare check.

During this time Sergeant Wall had thankfully left the team and Sergeant Sift became my team Sergeant.

My probation was extended due to Sergeant Wall's reports and recommendations which I felt were completely unfair. I discussed this with HR and informed them I believed Sergeant Wall was bullying me. We agreed that I could work on a different team and from a different Police station though on the same division. When I finally returned to work, I found out that Sergeant Wall had not documented my injury on duty, this was against protocol and I had no doubt it wasn't a mistake. I raised this issue to supervisors who tried to continually dismiss that it was an injury on duty, however I contacted HR and demanded it be completed.

. . .

I have no doubt this was to cover up the fact that I was already suffering an injury that prevented me from doing certain duties, because I was unable to wear my body armour and the fact that sergeant Wall put me in harms way with threats of not completing my probation. This is what the police do, if your face doesn't fit, if you challenge supervisors decisions and actions, they will go out of their way to make you look incompetent, they will try to cover things up, they are and always will be a boys club and you will only fit in with that if you adhere to their rules, if you say how high when they ask you to jump. I did not fit in with what they wanted, I challenged the boys club and they didn't like that.

FRESH START

It was my first day at my new station and I couldn't find my keys to the house or car, shit! I was searching for 30 minutes, before I found them down the sofa. I was now running late, I'm never late, it's one thing that really irritates me, I pride myself on being early so people aren't waiting on me. I loathe people being late as I find it disrespectful, this wasn't the impression I wanted to give to my new Sergeant's, I jumped in the car and went straight to my new police station Sandford South.

I'd missed parade, my new team were all in the writing room and I ran straight to the Sergeant's office. I was 20 minutes late and I felt like a little school girl heading to the head mistress's office. I entered the office and there I met my two new Sergeant's, Sgt Harp and Sgt Ealing, they clearly weren't impressed. Sergeant Ealing was a tall muscular guy, he looked like Mr Incredible, he had a steely look on his face, I felt intimidated, Sergeant Harp was smaller both in height and stature but had the look of disappointment, that felt worse than the intimidation as I don't like to disappoint.

They both gave me the third degree, I was so embarrassed. This was not the impression I wanted to make. They were aware of my probation being extended and we had a discussion regarding that, Sergeant Harp was to be my team Sergeant and one I would report to most. I was told what was expected of me and because I was coming back from an injury and wasn't out of my probation, they wanted me to be partnered with a tutor for the first couple of weeks, I was fine with that, her name was PC Jays and I was sent to find her.

As I walked to the main writing room, I passed the secondary writing room and was met with an "Ay Up" and a huge smile, "Hello" I replied with a smile. The "Ay Up meaning Hello, came from Jack Hill, he was handsome, with a huge smile and big blue eyes, he was muscular too, it was the first time I had smiled all morning. I entered the writing room where I met some of my new team, I asked if anyone could tell me where my patrol partner was, that's where I met PC Jays and off out on patrol we went. When the day finally ended, and I was happy it was over.

Over the coming weeks I got to know PC Jays well, she was a great police officer. I really liked the team, they were fun and hardworking and a most importantly they all had morals and were good police officers, I felt I fitted in well and for the first time since I became a police officer, I really enjoyed the job and understood what they meant by you become a family.

After a couple of weeks partnered with PC Jays I was partnered with PC Hill and we became regular van partners, and as the cliché goes, before long we started dating. I had recently come out of a relationship and didn't feel ready for another, so we were off and on to start with, but Jack persisted and before long we were dating properly.

As van partners and before we were dating, Jack had told me he didn't want marriage or children and this was something I wasn't willing to compromise on, I've always imagined getting married and having children, so within the first few weeks of dating I asked Jack out right if he wanted these things because if he didn't I wasn't going to waste either of our time dating and we should just go our separate ways now. However, Jack told me that since he had met me, the love of his life, he had changed his mind and wanted marriage and children and he wanted those things with me.

Things were going really well with Jack, he was funny, confident, outgoing, he was constantly telling me how beautiful I was and before long he invited me to meet his family at his cousins 21st birthday party. I already had prior commitments so I arrived a little later than everyone else. I was incredibly nervous, not only was I meeting his mum and Dad for the first time but his siblings, cousins, aunties, uncles I was being thrown in at the deep end as everyone was going to be there.

The party was at his mum and Dads house. As I was driving down his mum's street, I phoned Jack to ask which was the house and before I knew it I slammed on my brakes as a male came running out of a driveway onto the road waving at me to stop, I stopped in time and he put his hands on the bonnet of my car and directed me into the driveway laughing and there was Jack. As I got out of my car Jack introduced me to his brother Seth, he was the idiot I nearly knocked over, he was quite drunk, but I wasn't surprised as he was drinking pints of vodka.

We went into the back garden where there was a marquee and a party in full swing, Jack was introducing me to different people, and I sat on a chair and began talking to Jack's uncle who was such a lovely man, the next thing I heard was a woman's voice shouting.

"Get me the heater Philip".

I see a man fiddling with some wires and trying to move a large outside heater.

"Fucking hell Philip, just hurry up".

. . .

"I'm trying Jane" he replied, and with that this small middle-aged woman jumped up from her seat.

"If I want anything doing around here, I need to do it my fucking self, move Philip" she shouted.

Oh, how delightful I thought as Jack asked me to come inside the house to get a drink.

We went into the house and you immediately entered the kitchen from the back garden, Jack opened the fridge and got me a drink of diet Pepsi, as his Dad came into the kitchen from another room in the house.

Jack introduced me to his Dad, it was Philip and he gave me a kiss on the cheek and said, "Hello". Philip was a very smiley man and I could see where Jack got his big smile from, he seemed kind and was a funny man.

I met his sister Sue who was a large bubbly girl and very excited to meet me, she couldn't tell me enough about how much Jack was in love with me and that he had never brought a girl home before. It was incredibly sweet of her and my initial thoughts were how lovely and sweet she seemed, I was looking forward to getting to know her.

. . .

Then I noticed Jane, the same woman I heard shouting at Philip, Jack's Dad in the garden had also come into the kitchen, though she had a face like thunder.

"Mum, this is Helen" Jack said.

"I'm busy son" she replied with a scowl as she looked at me and walked out of the kitchen into the back garden. No one apologised or addressed her rudeness and the conversation continued as if nothing was wrong. We finally got introduced later in the evening, by then she was drunk, rude, foul mouthed and uncouth, so my first impression of his mum wasn't a good one and my gut was telling me we may not get on.

Back at work things were going really well, I would have regular meetings with my sergeants and to their surprise they couldn't believe I was the same person who they were told would be joining the team. Aside from the first day I was always early and ready for shift, my standard of work was high, my performance was great and they had absolutely no complaints, they pointed out if this was continued I would breeze through my extended probation and they were really happy to have me as part of the team, not only were my sergeants happy but they informed me the team were happy with me too, they believed I fitted in well. This made me realise I was a good police officer and confirmed what I already thought, Sergeant Wall was bullying me but for what reason I will never know.

I enjoyed going to work and I was flying through my extended probation, the meetings with my sergeants were always positive and before long I was confirmed in rank.

Unfortunately, my time at this station came to an abrupt end, it became public knowledge that I had started dating Jack, we kept it quiet from our supervisors for as long as we possibly could, however his jealous ex who was a civilian in the station had begun to cause trouble for us, making up lies and false accusations. She was married when she was having her affair with Jack and when her husband found out about the affair he kept contacting Jack and threatening him, her husband I might add, was also a police officer.

During the investigation of her allegations it was found she had been lying, saying she was in work when cctv showed she had not been in on some of those days. Because she was emigrating they decided to allow her to leave with no consequences. Unfortunately for me this meant I had to be moved, I went back to Sandford North police station though still on the same shift pattern just a different station on the north of the division and a different team. I was gutted, I really liked the South team, not a single one of them was unethical, they all worked hard, and we had great team cohesion and camaraderie. So I was sad to leave.

. . .

My first day with the Sandford North team was good, I knew a number of them already as my older team overlapped this team previously so that was nice. They were very welcoming and I soon enjoyed working with them. There were however two officers on the team that were having an affair, Pat was married, and Jen was single.

It was a well known relationship within the division, this was because they made no secret to meeting up at stations and engaging in sexual activities, no one seemed to bat an eyelid. They were often caught coming out of various offices and rooms in a state of undress. On nights out, they were quite open about their relationship even in the presence of supervision so I was surprised that they were allowed to continue working together even when supervision were aware of such ongoing conduct.

This was not the only occurrence of sexual outrage within the team, following a Christmas team night out, a female member of staff reported she had been raped. As you can imagine we were mortified that this had happened, a number of officers and staff members were spoken to about the night out and it soon transpired the member of staff had engaged in consensual sexual activity with another male and made the false allegation of rape because she was married and didn't want to tell her husband the truth. This female actually kept her job within the force.

One Saturday evening when I was leaving work I had

excruciating stomach pains, it was so bad I had to go to the hospital, whilst there they sent me to the gynaecology unit as the pain was in my pelvis and vaginal area. They wanted to put me on some antibiotics as they believed it could be a urinary tract infection and it would be better to start treatment than wait for the results first.

However they needed to do a pregnancy test in order to rule pregnancy out because of the antibiotics, I laughed and said it will be negative as I was on the pill, however when the nurse came back with the results, she confirmed I was in actual fact pregnant, I was shocked and I think I went through every possible emotion within a 10 minute period.

All I remember saying is I can't be pregnant; we haven't got a house! I wanted to get married and have a house first before we welcomed children in to the world. At 25 years of age, I was still so young, because of the pain I was experiencing, the Dr now thought I might be suffering with an ectopic pregnancy, because it was the weekend, they were unable to perform a scan on me until Monday and I would therefore have to stay in hospital. I was in such a state of upset and confusion, the nurse contacted Jack for me. Jack came straight from work to the hospital and we told him the news, I could see straight away he wasn't happy, but he was more concerned about my health.

The following morning whilst sat next to me in the hospital bed, we discussed the pregnancy, Jack told me he wasn't happy about it but we would make it work and he then called his mum to cancel our plans with her that day and informed her that we were pregnant.

"How could you be so fucking stupid" she shouted down the phone, I was completely taken aback by her reaction.

"You have only been together for a year" she continued.

Jack explained the circumstances and ended the call.

Monday soon came around and the scan showed the pregnancy was not ectopic and baby was growing exactly where it should. I was elated as I had finally got my head around being pregnant. I had to go back for a scan a couple of weeks later, however on this occasion I was told the babies heartbeat was irregular and I should come back in a week. Upon my return there was no change with the irregular heartbeat and this time the heartbeat was slowing down, I was informed the pregnancy was not viable and the baby would die.

They gave me the option of allowing the baby to die and expel naturally but they didn't know how long that would take or I could have a procedure to terminate the pregnancy, my heart was broken but I decided to have the pregnancy terminated, I couldn't wait for my baby to slowly die inside of me. I was booked in for the procedure and told Jack he would need to be with me, he informed work of the circumstances and he was refused the leave to be with me, I was furious, how could they do this, it was short notice but I was losing my baby, I needed him there.

Finally, he went in to work and demanded the time off and he was with me on that awful day. As you can imagine, it was a distressing time for me and I took some time off work. When I went back to work on recuperative duties, they placed me in the public service team, the same place they put the ladies that are pregnant and at that time there were a three who were pregnant.

During this time we had put an offer in on a house and had decided to move to his parent's house for a few weeks to save a little more money prior to moving into our new house and one evening following dinner Jane and I were sat at the table in the kitchen, Jane had consumed a few alcoholic drinks which wasn't uncommon as she liked her drink, Jack was in the living room with Philip when Jane started telling me how lucky I was to be with Jack, I was biting my tongue and trying not to respond negatively, when Jane started saying she hated me because I'd treated her son like a piece of shit at the start of our relationship, I tried to politely tell her that she wasn't aware of the circumstances and reasoning behind our on again off again start to the relationship when she turned to me and said,

. . .

"If I'd had a knife, I'd have stabbed you".

I couldn't believe the words that had just come out of her mouth, I was completely gob smacked then Jack came into the kitchen, he saw the look on my face and asked me if I was ok, I told him I wasn't and that I was going to bed and he said he would be up later. I was lying in bed still in shock of the words that I just heard his mother say to me, did she really hate me that much and for what reason, I haven't been anything but polite to her.

I was still awake when Jack came to bed, as he lay next to me I turned to him and said I needed to talk to him, he asked me what was wrong? I told him what his mum had said to me and that I think he should speak to her about it as it had really upset me. She was just drunk he responded, you know how she gets. I still want you to talk to her as it's a very nasty thing to say, he continued to try and justify his mums behaviour. I told him I won't be spoken to like that by his mum and he needs to address it.

"Shut up" he responded.

"I don't get why you don't see a problem with what your mum has said to me" I said.

. . .

"Shut up, they're only next door" he snapped only this time he elbowed me so hard in the ribs.

I was stunned at what he had just done to me, tears rolled down my face whilst I held the area Jack had just hurt. In the same night his mum had been verbally abusive to me and the man I loved had been physically abusive to me.

I had so much going through my head, we were going on a family holiday in a few weeks and we had just bought a house that we were due to move into when we got back, we'll lose so much money, what should I do.

"Don't ever do that again because I'll walk" I said through my tears, Jack rolled over and fell asleep, whilst I cried myself to sleep.

I woke early the next morning Jack was still sleeping, my ribs were in so much pain and as I looked down, I could see the distinct bruising where Jack had hurt me. I lay in bed with so many thoughts running through my head, it wasn't long before Jack woke up. He didn't want to talk about what had happened the night before and he didn't want to discuss what his mum had said either. When we went down for breakfast his mum also didn't mention what had occurred the previous night.

. . .

As we were moving in to our own home in few weeks and going on holiday with the whole family, I decided to try and forget about the whole evening.

I enjoyed working in the public service team though it wasn't without incident, we had a male colleague Pc Toft who was a little peculiar to say the least, he had started to date one of my other colleagues' sister. The relationship soon ended. However, a few weeks later we were sat in the office when PC Toft jumped up from his chair and said he didn't feel well, and could we let supervision know he was going home.

As he went to leave the office two males stopped him as he was leaving, they introduced them self as internal investigation officers and arrested Pc Toft, we were in complete shock. It turned out PC Toft had been using a police vehicle whilst on duty to harass his ex girlfriend, stalk her outside her house and even record himself masturbating in the police vehicle outside her house and then sent her the video. PC Toft had been using the police systems to check if she had reported him to the police.

Just before he was arrested, he had seen on the police system that she had reported him and that the officers were currently on their way to arrest him, hence his sudden sickness and urge to leave. Upon investigation it also became apparent that PC Toft had possession of extreme animal pornography on both his phone and laptop.

. . .

All the other charges were dropped but he was found guilty in court for possession of extreme pornography and he subsequently resigned from the police force. This wasn't the first time PC Toft had been in trouble, he was caught closing and finalising crimes as offenders arrested and crime detected without actually arresting and interviewing anyone. He also wasn't the only officer who was found to be doing this.

UNLAWFUL POLICE

After several months in the public service team I submitted a request to go to Sandford Middle neighbourhood team. I had an informal interview with the inspector who I had always got on well with. I was notified on the day I would be accepted it was just the formalities of HR.

I was glad to start working with the neighbourhood team in Sandford middle, they had a great inspector and I was looking forward to being back out on the streets again.

As neighbourhood officers we were all assigned our own neighbourhood, the busier areas had more officers. I had a relatively quiet area but I enjoyed it all the same. Working in the neighbourhood team was great to start with, as long as you worked hard and did what was asked of you, you were left to it. However, for some reason, the powers that be decided they wanted to move our inspector to a different unit, they didn't like the way he ran the neighbourhood team anymore, this happened despite it being an award winning team, it must have been a personal grudge against him because he wasn't a yes sir, no sir type.

It wasn't long after I joined the neighbourhood team that Jack proposed, I was delighted to be getting married and it was the most romantic Jack had ever been. He proposed on Valentine's Day, with champagne, flowers, gifts, breakfast in bed and my beautiful ring, I wasn't expecting it though we had been together for over three years, of course I said yes and I couldn't wait to show my friends the ring and start planning our wedding.

During my time at Sandford middle I met a homeless man name Colin, he had a dog who was his world and he would do anything for her. Colin was an alcoholic who had been living on the streets for quite a number of years, and because of this he was often in Sandford middle town centre begging for money, because of this behaviour he had various antisocial behavioural orders (ASBO) against him.

One of the conditions of his ASBO was that he was not allowed to be in Sanford middle town centre begging, if he did, he would be in beach of this ASBO and subsequently arrested. I hated that he had this condition on his ASBO, he had no home and no means of income or benefits, so this was how he fed himself and his dog, we were further punishing someone who was already suffering. Just because it's the law doesn't mean it's right.

Whenever a call came in regarding Colin, I would always try to get to the location before any other officer and use my discretion, not arrest him although I would remove him from the location with a warning, on some occasions when it was a quiet night I would buy some food for Colin and his dog Meghan and let them get warm in my vehicle, even have a sleep until I was called to another incident.

On numerous occasions other officers would get to the scene before I did. On one particular occasion as I was arriving at the location I noticed another police van pull up just before me and Colin was trying to run away, I saw my colleague Jeff jump out of the van as Colin was running past him, he punched him to the floor, then jumped on top of Colin and continued to hit him, whilst calling him a barrage of derogatory names. I told Jeff to get the fuck off him and there was no possible reason for him to treat Colin in this way.

Jeff's reply was that he was a piece of shit, he then arrested Colin and dragged him into the van.

I was then sent to deal with other incidents, I later went back to my station to speak with my sergeant, I went to his office and found him asleep at his desk, I knocked on the door loudly and he woke up asking what I wanted. I informed him about what I had witnessed, he told me that Jeff had already spoken to him and the force used was necessary to arrest Colin and if I continued to make accusations of this nature, I would make myself enemies very quickly. I tried to argue that it wasn't appropriate, and Sergeant Abbas told me we were a team and we were supposed to stick together and if I didn't like it, I was in the wrong job. I walked away shaking my head, this was the start of a fractious relationship.

Soon we were informed that each officer had to have a minimum of four arrests and four detections each month. This meant every officer had to make a minimum of four arrests for separate offences and have four crimes solved (detected) if this target was not reached, steps would be taken to put the officer on an action plan. They also wanted officers to submit a certain number of stop and search forms too. Their reasoning behind this was it was a way to show proactive policing.

It was a ridiculous idea, you can't measure a police officer's performance based on how many arrests and detections they have or how many stop and search forms they submit. All police roles are different and as a neighbourhood officer, you deal with a lot of neighbour disputes for instance, that take up a lot of time often with no arrests or crimes being committed. I knew exactly what was going to happen and sure enough I was proved right.

. . .

Most of the team at Sandford middle were hard working and good police officers, I enjoyed working with a lot of them, however there were the odd ones who were lazy and who thought because they wore a uniform, they could do what they wanted and treat people how they wanted and they didn't play by the rule book.

I found that the latter officers would not be getting the required amount of arrests and detection each month so come the end of the month they were antagonising people in order to get an easy arrest and detection, they were also stopping and searching people without the appropriate grounds to do so.

One weekend whilst on a late shift, I was walking through Sandford middle town centre with my colleague Dean, when a small group of four males whistled at me, they were slightly intoxicated but doing no harm, it's the nature of the job being a woman in uniform.

"Can I have your number officer?" shouted one of them as we walked past.

I laughed and told him the only number he would get would be my collar number should I have cause to arrest him.

They laughed and I got the traditional responses, "You can

put me in cuffs any day love" and "You can arrest me anytime officer".

I laughed but Dean told them to "wind your fucking necks in".

As we started to walk away one of them said to his friend, "What's his problem?".

And with that Dean turned around went over to them, "Say that again" he said in an aggressive tone.

Telling them they were not fucking big enough to say it to his face.

Dean then decided he wanted to search him, to which he was refusing and asking what the search was for.

I tried to reason with Dean, the guys were just having fun and he had no lawful or reasonable grounds to search him, at this point Dean decided he could smell drugs and that formed the grounds for his search. I couldn't smell drugs on them. Dean asked me to search the other males but I refused saying I didn't believe we have the grounds to search them. Dean searched them anyway and as expected he didn't find any drugs.

. . .

He told them next time keep their fucking mouths shut. As he walked over to me, he said he needed those stop and searches to keep the sergeants off his arse. I told him he'd conducted unlawful searches and couldn't just fabricate the smell of drugs.

A few weeks later, I was partnered with Dean again when an incident came over the radio that a personal robbery had just occurred, the perpetrators description was a black male, late teens, wearing black bottoms and a black hoody with the hood up, had robbed a victim on his pushbike and stole a mobile phone.

A patrol was already with the victim so Dean and I were in the area conducting a search for the perpetrator, when I noticed a lone person with their back to me in all black clothing walking down the street to my left, I told Dean to turn left and as we pulled up to the person I noticed the person was a black female.

I wound the window down and asked her if she had seen a black male acting suspiciously or looking as if he was running away from someone, she told me she had not and asked why, I told her a robbery had just taken place and she should be careful, I said thank you but Dean ignored me and pulled the vehicle over to speak with the female.

. . .

I asked what he was doing, he said the person looked like a male, I tried to reason with him, she was quite evidently a female, however he got out of the car and walked onto the pavement to the female and started to ask her questions, asking her where she had been and where she was going. She asked what the problem was when Dean told her she fitted the description of someone who had just committed the robbery. Quite rightly she replied you just told me that was a male, I am a female why have you stopped me?

"You're fucking black and look like a male" replied Dean

The female was quite upset at being stopped and didn't hold back in telling Dean so, he was clearly provoking the female telling the her it wasn't his fault she looked like a male then threatened to arrest her for public order. As Dean said this I heard over the radio that the perpetrator had been arrested.

I told Dean the male had been arrested and to let her go home. I apologised to the female for the inconvenience gave her my details and told her if she wanted to make a complaint I would back her, she took my details but I never heard anything more. Dean got in the vehicle and we left, I told him he was out of order and I could clearly tell the person was female and he started laughing saying they all look the same.

"What the fuck does that mean?" I spat furiously.

. . .

He just laughed, I felt disgusted that he was a police officer.

The next day I spoke to my Sergeant Abbas about Dean and he said he would handle it but it was never mentioned again.

A few weeks later Sergeant Abbas asked for a patrol to come and assist him, it was early evening but dark and cold as it was late autumn. Dean and I were in a vehicle together and went to assist the sergeant, upon arrival the sergeant and another colleague Jeff were with a small group of about six black males in their mid teens. They barely looked like they had gone through puberty.

As we got out of the car the sergeant asked us to search the males, "On what grounds were we to search them?" I asked.

"Just search them" was the sergeant's response.

"I need to know on what grounds sarge" I said, "I'm giving you a lawful order and if you don't follow it" he replied.

"Sorry Sarge, if I'm not given any lawful grounds in which to search the male, I won't be searching them" I said.

. . .

I could see that Dean and Jeff looking at me with a look of disgust on their faces as they were searching the males.

"Just search them for drugs Helen" said the sergeant.

"I don't believe I have lawful grounds to search hem for drugs sarge" I replied.

"If you want to search them that's fine but I'm not searching them and putting my name on a stop search form if I don't believe I have the grounds for the search" I continued.

"Just go and get in the vehicle Helen, I want to see you in my office later" he said furiously.

I walked away and got in to the vehicle, about ten minutes later Dean got in the vehicle with me.

"Tut tut tut tut tut" Dean said. "What?" I said.

He then told me I was never going to get far in the police challenging authority, I have no ambition to climb the ranks

I informed him, he continued to tell me that they would make my life hell if I didn't do what they asked.

"There were no grounds to search them Dean" I snapped.

"They were black, that's the grounds" he said laughing.

"You're a fucking racist piece of shit Dean" I said furious.

He laughed, telling me I was too sensitive for this job.

I ignored him, I couldn't help but think how there are so many awful police officers, these boys were kids and had been singled out and searched because of the colour of their skin. I'm not in the police for an easy life I thought, I just want to do a good lawful job at the end of the day and as long as I know I have done my best I can sleep easy at night.

However the unethical behaviours from others officers was troubling. Drugs were the easiest grounds for officers to search people at will, if the officer wanted to do an unlawful search, they would say the smelt drugs.

We headed to a few more incidents and returned to the

station, Sergeant Abbas asked me to go and speak with him in his office.

I entered the office, he told me to close the door and sit. "I'm ok standing thank you" I replied as I closed the door.

"Don't you ever challenge me again, when I ask you to do something you do it, do you understand?" he barked whilst pointing at me.

"No, I don't, if you give me a lawful order to follow, I will do it, however I don't believe I had the grounds to search those males earlier, you didn't give me a valid reason as to why they needed searching" I said.

"We are a team here at Sandford middle Helen, that means we stick together, and we work together to keep the team's results excellent" he said.

"I'm not going to search someone just because they are black, its racist, you are racist" I said, I could feel my face burning.

He then said if I didn't like it, that maybe Sandford middle wasn't the team for me.

. . .

"Can I go now?" I said, my shift was coming to an end and I needed to update the systems before I left.

"Go, and make sure you don't leave before you have updated your crimes and things" he said.

I turned and walked out of his office.

Below are my forces stop search statistics, we are one of the largest police forces in the country, these statistics are based on actual stop search documents handed in and submitted. There are numerous times I have witnessed officers not giving the paperwork to the person stopped and searched and numerous times officers haven't even bothered to fill out the paperwork. My force does not keep a record of stop accounts which I can assure you happens an awful lot and the same goes for the stop account paperwork.

The police conducted 2,623 stop and searches under PACE Section 1 across the area covered by Sandford police force. This was a reduction of 0.1% from the previous year.

Stop and account

Sandford Police do not record stop and accounts.

. . .

What are searches targeted at?

Target - Proportion of searches

Drugs - 47%

Offensive weapons - 27%

Stolen property - 13%

Going equipped - 9%

Firearms -2%

Other - 1%

Criminal damage - 1%

How effective are police stop and searches?

April 2017 – March 2018

11% of stop and searches conducted under PACE Section 1 lead to an arrest.

Who is getting searched?

Disproportionality has continued to creep upwards in Sandford for some racial groups, despite a fall in the overall number of recorded stop and searches within the city and nationally.

In 2017/18, black people were searched at almost five times

the rate of whites; Asians were searched at almost two and a half times the rate of whites, both increases on the previous year.

Mixed race people were searched at two and a half times the rate of whites; it was 3.2 times in the previous year. Those classified as being from Chinese or other ethnicities were searched at little over half the rate of whites.

Only a single search was conducted under section 60, a power that does not require officers to suspect people of criminality before detaining them for a search. Previously, nine searches were recorded under this power.

(Stopwatch.org) 2019

PACE disproportionality ratios

Ethnic groups Ratio

White : Black 1 : 4.7

White : Asian 1 : 2.4

White : Mixed 1 : 2.5

White : Other 1 : 0.6

(Stopwatch.org) 2019

From my experience and the above statistics, the fact of the matter is, black and Asian males have a target on their backs from the moment they leave their home, it's blatant discrimination and this needs to change. Stop search powers are misused, they target black and Asian males disproportionately, they undermine community relations and are ineffective at reducing crime.

The new relaxed powers making it easier for officers to impose a section 60 powers of the Criminal Justice and Public Order Act 1994, which allows them to search any person in a designated area, for a set amount of time if it is feared there is a likelihood of serious violence, allowing police in England and Wales to stop search people without "reasonable suspicion" in the attempt to tackle knife crime it is only going to exacerbate an already discriminatory system and plays right into police prejudice.

Victims of illegal stop searches will complain to police but officers sometimes do not complete the mandatory stop search form and submit it, they purposefully do not tell the control room they are conducting a stop search or check a persons details on the local and national database resulting in no record of the search taking place and no evidence to show police discrimination towards black and Asian persons is in fact higher than recorded.

POLICE MANIPULATION

I was sat in the writing room at Sandford middle going through all my crimes on the computer, I had been off for a couple of rest days and I was making my to do list. My colleague Kelly was sat next to me,

"There have been a few thefts from McColl's by a male offender" Kelly said.

"Is he Asian by any chance?" I asked.

"That's a racist comment" said Sergeant Abbas from behind me.

"Erm…. No, it's not Sarge, I'm just" I said before he cut me off;

. . .

"My office" he snapped not allowing me to finish what I was saying and walking away.

I looked at Kelly, "What the fuck is his problem?" she said, I rolled my eyes and went to his office.

He spat his usual bark of shut the door and sit when I entered, "I'm ok standing thanks" I responded whilst shutting the door, seems to be regular start to our conversation when I enter his office, I thought to myself.

"You come to my office making accusations against your colleagues yet you yourself make a racist comment" he spat.

"No Sarge, if you" I tried to say before he cut me off again.

"I don't expect that sort of behaviour from one of my officers" he snapped.

I'm stood in front of this sorry excuse of a male, my face burning because I would love to tell him what I really thought of him, but I keep calm and remain professional.

. . .

"If you actually allowed me to finish what I started to say in the writing room and just now, you would have heard I am currently dealing with numerous crimes at the same store for an Asian male offender, hence me asking if this offender was Asian, no racist intent at all" I said.

"Don't let me hear you come out with something like that again" he replied.

"Are we done?" I asked.

"You can go" he said without even looking at me.

I turned and left his office, clearly, he wasn't happy with me, not only for challenging his authority regarding what I believed to be illegal searches but also for speaking out about both Dean and Jeff's actions.

In the police force, every crime has a definition for each offence to be proved, this means each offence has points that have to be proven for the offender to be charged with said offence.

The offence of robbery has the following definition

. . .

"A person is guilty of robbery if he steals, and immediately before or at the time of doing so, and in order to do so, he uses force on any person or puts or seeks to put any person in fear of being then and there subjected to force "

For an offender to be charged with robbery we have to make sure all of the above is proven. Unfortunately, on numerous occasions within the police force I along with other officers were told to manipulate the way we wrote up the modus operandi (MO) of how the crime was committed, this was so we could manipulate the crime figures within the area and make it look like we were having less robberies than we actually were.

We were therefore told to put robbery offences in as theft and assault crimes making the robbery figures look better than they actually were. These were not the only figures that were manipulated, we were told where possible not to submit crimes, subsequently making the crime figures as a whole look like they were dropping, we just had to make sure we wrote the incident update in a manner that would support this as no crime.

Another type of figure that officers used to manipulate was something called TIC procedure (taken into consideration), this is where there is sufficient evidence to charge a person with an offence, then consideration must be applied for capture of any further like offences by way of TIC procedure. This apples for all suspects admitting to offences in interview and provisions should be considered for offenders at court of other locations wishing to accept TIC.

The Police and Criminal Evidence Act 1984 (PACE) gives provisions to interview suspects for offences other than those which resulted in the initial arrest, as long as there are reasonable grounds for suspecting the offender's involvement in those offences.

On countless occasions, I witnessed offenders being arrested and then being told to also admit to further like offences, this was even before we had got to the custody suite. It was known as "wording them up".

They were told things like "you're already going back to prison, you may as well admit to this offence and these other ones too, the court will be more lenient on you for doing so".

"We've had a number of thefts / robberies similar to this, you are already admitting to this so you may as well say you did these too, it would benefit you at court".

"Look, you've never been in trouble with cops before, say you have done these too, you will get a lesser punishment for assisting police".

. . .

It was even used in a positive light for an offender that was happy to go back to prison if he was homeless. He was told if he admitted these other offences, he would get a longer prison sentence and in turn a bed and meals provided for longer whilst serving his time in prison.

This list goes on and on for the rationale officers would give offenders. This was done so officers could have more crimes detected, once again manipulating the figures to look like more crime was being solved, when in actual fact, it was lies. Not only did this make the division look like it was solving crimes, it made the force crime detection rates look good and therefore the national statistics look positive too. Just because someone has committed a previous crime does not justify officers coercing them into confessing to other crimes when they are innocent of them purely for the benefit of police officer and force statistics.

Every force has many prolific offenders and my force was no different. Part of being a police officer is gathering intelligence, this can be done in a variety of ways. This was part of the job I enjoyed, building a rapport with individuals and gathering intelligence, there was however ways the division gathered intelligence that I disagreed with. We had a traffic light system check list, this was a list of offenders that the division wanted to keep a watchful eye over.

The 'red' offenders were those who were either recently released from prison and required to wear an electronic tagging device which is a method of electronic surveillance in the form of an ankle monitor worn by the offender, and offenders who had curfews and or bail conditions imposed by the courts or police.

These offenders all had time restrictions imposed on them to be at a required location during specific times. Because of this we were required to attend the designated location every night to check the offender was adhering to their tag, bail and curfew conditions. Intelligence was then updated and if the offender was not present a statement would be completed by the attending officers for the breach of conditions to enable an arrest to take place.

The "amber" offenders were those who were prolific offenders or offenders we had current intelligence that they were currently active in committing crimes but had no electronic tagging device or bail/curfew conditions. We were told to attend the homes and known addresses of these persons every other day, the purpose of this was to give a time and location the person was seen by a police officer or if the offender was not present, and to get a current description of the person and to document what clothing they were wearing at that time.

The "green" offenders were persons known to the police for specific crimes and we were to attend their home address at least once a week, again to document time and location the person was seen by a police officer, and a description of the offenders and their clothing. It was also to make the offenders know that we were keeping an eye on them.

The unfortunate thing about this system is it was abused, officers were using it to harass offenders, sometimes knocking on the 'red' light offenders address more than once a night and if it wasn't the offender opening the door, they would tell the person who did to go and wake the offender and get them out of bed and present themselves to the officer.

The same was happening with the "amber" and "green" offenders, officers were attending their homes on more occasions than they should have done. As you can imagine the offenders on the list and their families were not too happy about this, but the officers were enjoying the fact that they were harassing the offenders, purposefully doing so in order to get a reaction from them in the hope to get an easy arrest.

Some of the families even contacted the police station to report this unfair treatment, but these complaints as many complaints from the public are, were swept under the carpet and nothing is done about them. In fact, when some of these complaints did in actual fact come in, we were told to "Piss them off" make sure we attended their address on that day, and subsequent days and to make sure they knew if they commit crime in our area, we will harass them.

. . .

Now don't get me wrong, if you commit a crime, I do believe you should be punished for that crime, however, I don't agree with police abusing their position to harass offenders and their family. We are not above the law, we are there to uphold the law.

POLICE PREJUDICE

I was looking forward to getting married in October of this year, I had been planning it for a while and it hadn't been an easy process to start with, we always said we would get married abroad in 2010, but Jack's mum and sister took umbrage to this because they would have to pay to be there, we assured them we would assist as it would be cheaper to get married abroad but we were continually met with their objections, Jack's sister had also decided to get married in 2010 and didn't like the fact we were too.

So, Jack said he would only marry me if we got married in the UK, I was devastated at first I remembered my dream as a little girl wanting my family there so I could understand his feelings. So, we settled on Rookery Hall in Nantwich, it was a beautiful grade II listed Elizabethan style mansion which dates back to 1816, once we had a look around

Rookery Hall we both knew this was the place, we left that day with our wedding booked for Friday, October 1st, 2010

With the venue and date set, the next big thing to find was my wedding dress, all the ideas I'd previously had were no longer suitable for an autumn wedding, so I went looking with an open mind. I went shopping for my wedding dress on my own, everything I thought I would like, I didn't once it was on, so when I went to a quaint little bridal boutique in Cheshire, I was expecting another disappointing day.

The owner was a lovely lady called Hayley so I should have known it would be a great day right there. She was so welcoming and warm, she asked me if I was expecting anyone to join me and my heart sank, I felt a little embarrassed when I informed her I was on my own and for the first time in a long time my eyes filled with tears and I wished more than anything I had my mum or Dad with me to share this with.

Hayley noticed my sadness and brought me some tissues and said a few kind words. I then chose a few dresses and tried them on and once again I was getting disappointed, Hayley then said she had the perfect dress for my figure, when she brought me the dress, I wasn't too keen on it, but she was the professional and out of kindness I wanted to try it on.

. . .

When I looked in the mirror it was beautiful, not a dress I would have chosen but perfect for me. I felt beautiful in it, yet I couldn't hide my sadness and disappointment at having no one to share the moment with, though I was happy I had found my dress and ordered it the same day.

I enjoyed planning our wedding, Jack was happy to let me get on with the planning and make the decisions though it was nice to take him along to have a look at my ideas. I wanted it simple and elegant, black and white, with white avalanche roses, calla lilies and candles everywhere.

We had planned to go to Scotland for a long weekend over the Easter bank holiday to go shopping with one of my bridesmaids Michelle for her bridesmaid dress. We intended to go from Friday to Monday and had this planned for months. I was at court the week beforehand, so I was not working my original shifts when I received an email from Sergeant Moss telling me he had cancelled my Saturday rest day to provide police visibility at a community summer fair.

This fair had been planned months in advance, and is a yearly event so to only get a few days' notice that my rest day was cancelled and, and that they knew I had plans to go away for the weekend ad this further added to my beliefs that they were treating me unfairly. It wasn't as if I minded working the summer fairs, you get to meet the people within your community, enjoy summer games with them and eat ice cream, who wouldn't enjoy that as a day's work.

I contacted Sergeant Moss to inform him of my plans, to which I was told I would be working the fair and he had the power to cancel my rest days as and when he deemed fit. I was so annoyed, I decided to contact my federation rep who was as much use as a chocolate fireguard. He told me I needed to prove I was going to Scotland but as I was staying at our friend's house and driving in my car, I had no documents to show this trip was already booked in advance.

I again spoke with Sergeant Moss and I tried to reason with him, I informed him I had no other weekends that we could do this due to work commitments and other wedding plans being made, I made him aware we were already in April and the wedding was only six months away, therefore this was something I needed to get confirmed this weekend. I was told if I did not work this I would be disciplined. I tried so hard to negotiate with him, I asked if he could ask someone else to take my place and again, I was told I if I didn't work it, I would be disciplined. I wouldn't have minded so much if it was the Friday or the Monday as we could have gone to Scotland later or returned home earlier but it was the Saturday right in the middle of the long weekend making it impossible.

I decided to go to see the new inspector, I didn't have much luck there either, she informed me Sergeant Moss could cancel my rest days and she stood by his decision. It didn't surprise to me that she stood by his decision, it was well known that they were now in a relationship and since this had happened, he was the one making most of the decisions around the station, not her.

I went in to the office where the rest of my colleagues were and by this time most of them were aware of the circumstances, I had numerous colleagues volunteer to work the shift for me. With that information, I walked back to the inspector's office and told her as there were a number officers who were willing to work the shift instead of me, it was unfair for them to force me to do it and discipline me should I refuse to work it due to prearranged commitments. I could tell she was furious with me but agreed that would be a satisfactory outcome then informed me I would be working the next few summer fairs. I knew this wouldn't go down well but we had a wonderful weekend in Scotland with our friends and we managed to find a beautiful bridesmaids dress.

A lot of people in the police force do not like to be challenged, I knew that challenging Sergeant Moss and Inspector Bold meant things were not going to run smoothly with them for me. Sergeant Moss was known as the smiling assassin, he was already making one female officer's life a misery on the team, so much so she found herself buying him gifts to try and get him to change the way he treated her. So, it came as no surprise to me that our relationship would become difficult.

. . .

Not long after this incident I was sat in the police station completing paper work when I received a point to point, this is like a telephone call via your personal issue radio.

It was Sergeant Moss "Where are you?".

"I'm in the police station".

Moss "You're lying, I can see you are not in the police station".

"I am Sarge, I'm in my office doing paperwork" I responded, shocked at the accusation, "Why would you think I am lying?".

"I can see you are in Sandford Moor" he said,

"No Sarge, I'm in the station doing paperwork, I'll come up to your office" I replied.

It took me two minutes to walk up the stairs to the sergeant's office, "Sarge, see I'm in the office" I stated. As I did I could see the sergeant had the screen up on his computer of all the officers locations.

. . .

All of our radios had recently been updated with a GPS tracking device so the comms office could know each officers locations in case of an emergency and if back up was required, and to see who was closest to incidents for incident allocation and deployment. It was under no circumstances meant to be used for supervisors to be checking up on officer's locations and calling in to questions officers' integrity.

"Are you checking up on my location on that system?" I asked. "You can go and finish your paperwork now" he replied.

I took a deep breath, turned around shook my head as I walked away, clearly, he was breaking force policies, and it took everything I had in me not to say something more to him. I was getting married in six months and I didn't want any more rest days cancelled causing me problems with my plans.

A call came in of a domestic assault, it was unfortunately one of our regular female victims, I told comms I would attend and as I was leaving the station Dean shouted to me;

"Fucking leave the bitch, he may finally do us a favour and stop her from calling the police" he said laughing.

. . .

"Fuck off Dean" I snapped back.

"What?" he replied whilst laughing with some of the other male colleagues.

I attended the incident and the victim was heavily intoxicated and had been assaulted, the perpetrator was arrested but as always, the following morning the female would refuse to give a statement and the male would be released. It was so frustrating, this female was an alcoholic, I have no doubt it was her way of escaping, there was no support system to help her.

We continue to fail these victims, she is as much a victim of the system as she is a victim of domestic abuse and so she continued to be a victim of domestic abuse, and there was nothing I could do except turn up next time in the hope that she would still be alive and we can help her, and there will be a next time.

The unfortunate thing is there are many police officers I have worked with who have no empathy, they do not understand the psychology of abuse and see the victims as "asking for it" if they don't leave. It's a disgrace.

As expected, a few days later a call came in of a domestic

assault from the same female, she had reported the male had hit her with the butt of a gun.

I attended this address and Dean and Jeff arrived with me, as we alighted our vehicles Dean said, "He should have fucking shot her not hit her on the fucking head with it, that's how thick these bastards are".

"You're a dick Dean, imagine if this was your sister, mother etc…." I snapped. He laughed and mocked me.

I said I would speak with the female whilst Dean and Jeff spoke with the male. The female refused to tell me what had happened and kept saying she didn't like them, pointing to my colleagues Dean and Jeff.

Nothing I said could reassure her I could help, and unfortunately, we couldn't arrest the male, the gun was literally the butt of a gun so he couldn't be arrested for that either. I did however insist on removing the male from the property.

I have heard and challenged may derogatory comments from police officer in relation to many victims of crime. Here are just a few.

A prostitute was asking to be beaten and raped, she is a

whore it's what she does.

A domestic violence victim deserved to be beaten, I would beat her senseless too.

A male victim with a male partner was a victim of domestic abuse, he was told to man the fuck up homo.

A rape victim, officer asked who the fuck would rape her.

A black male robbery victim, who gives a shit he's black.

An Asian male was a terrorist because they are all the fucking same.

A particular area on our division was called Paki town.

ABUSE OF POSITION

We were doing our afternoon team briefing following a few rest days off, every shift starts with an officer reading out the briefing, during these briefings we are shown the latest wanted offenders, crimes and incidents that had occurred over the last few days and given our duties. During this briefing I was writing down the details of a wanted offender in my pocket note book when the details of another wanted offender appeared on the screen.

"Jacob Davis, a sex offender wanted on warrant for breaching his curfew." I heard my colleague say.

As I started to write the details in my note book, one of my colleagues shouted,

. . .

"Oh, is that your brother Helen, he looks like you" whilst they all laughed.

I looked up at the screen and it was in actual fact, my brother, his face was plastered across the briefing screen, a giant image of my brothers face with the words "SEX OFFENDER" written next to him, I was shocked and didn't know what to say, I felt physically sick, I had not been in contact with my family for a number of years so I had no idea that he had ever been arrested, let alone in prison, and for such a serious crime too.

I just laughed at them and tried not to let them know that it was indeed my brother. I could feel my eyes fill with tears, so I looked down to my pocket note book and pretended to write in it whilst gathering my thoughts, trying desperately not to allow any tears to roll down my cheeks. I didn't hear anything for the next few minutes of the briefing, fighting back the tears, tears of shame, tears of guilt, tears of embarrassment and tears of sympathy for the victim.

My mind was racing with so many unanswered questions. Who? What? Where? When? Why? And how? Who was his victim or were there more than one, my heart sank, thinking of the horrors my brother could have inflicted on someone, being a victim of sexual assault, myself aged 11 and 18 years, I knew how the victim could be feeling? The briefing ended and I immediately stood up and went in to my inspector's office, I asked if I could talk with her and closed the door, I informed her that Jacob Davis was my brother and I had no idea about any of this.

To my surprise, she was very understanding and sympathetic, she advised me she would need to take a few details from me and would request that the image be removed from our briefing. I couldn't apologise enough, however I think my apologies were more for his victim, rather than the inconvenience it was causing.

Inspector Bold assured me that this would remain between us and only those on a need to know basis would be informed. I was so thankful. I left her office to continue with my duties but I couldn't get rid of the nauseating feeling in the pit of my stomach, I wanted to know what my brother had done but I was also too scared to know, who wants to know that their sibling or anyone they are related to is capable of something so heinous. Throughout the day I couldn't stop thinking about my brother's victim. I knew I was going to have to do a Google search and look up this information, but I couldn't do it at work, I was too scared someone would see me googling "JACOB DAVIS" and realising the "JACOB DAVIS" in the briefing was my brother.

My shift ended and I got in my car ready to go home, I couldn't wait any longer, I took out my phone and googled my brothers details, my worst fears were realised, he was a paedophile, his victim was an 11 year old girl, as I read the newspaper reports I cried, his victim was the same age I was when a man tried to rape me.

How could my brother do such a thing, I was devastated, reading about the incident I saw it was the typical bullshit defence, they met online, she lied about her age, and to a point I get that, but once you know someone is under the consensual age? Bang. You stop. You walk away. You don't continue any sort of relationship, but he didn't, he continued to groom the young girl and tried to rape her and sexually assaulted her on more than one occasion, he is a paedophile and making excuses for his behaviour. His defence was she was a willing participant. His lawyer is just as disgusting as my brother, victim shaming, and blaming an eleven year old girl, he was wanted because he'd breached his bail conditions.

Things were becoming really difficult within the unit, I was constantly being reprimanded, having rest days cancelled which was making it difficult at work and for me to plan the wedding, I was being called into the sergeants office and reprimanded for petty things, including not saying good morning or hello when I walked past the sergeants office, for not being sociable with my sergeants, they were finding the smallest of issues to make things awkward for me. That coupled with the regular cancellation of rest days, Jack and I were getting no time off together. I was aware the response units were short on staff, so I put in a request to be moved to a response unit that had the same shift pattern as Jack did.

. . .

That didn't seem to go down well and one late shift I was asked to be on a scene, it was an outdoor scene, I didn't mind as it kept me away from supervision. However, after half the shift had gone by, nature was calling so I contacted Sergeant Abbas and asked if I could be relieved for a bathroom break, he told me we didn't have the staff free at the moment and he would sort it when he could, another thirty minutes went by and I had heard nothing, I contacted the sergeant again and he told me he would get someone to relieve me when free, I stressed to him that I was getting desperate and he cut me off.

It had been over an hour, I was in extreme pain trying not to pee my pants when I contacted the sergeant again, I told him I needed to be relieved urgently and once again, I was told to wait. I felt like he was doing this on purpose, I was in so much pain I could barely move, my eyes were filling with tears it was hurting that much, I wiggled myself to the farthest most covered part of the garden, fearing that every step my bladder was going to burst and I would pee myself, right there in my police uniform I had to crouch down relieve myself in the garden at a scene, I was furious but so glad to have relieved myself.

It's ok for a guy, they can relieve themselves in a bottle which many do, but for a female, it's a much more compromising position to relieve yourself, I was so worried I would be caught but I had no option. It was another two hours before someone was sent to relieve me.

During the wait process the team gained a new sergeant, Sergeant East, she was a colleague from the unit already and I had great respect for her, she was a great police officer, very fair and ethical so it was a great addition to the team. I was lucky enough to be give Sgt East as my Sergeant, she had witnessed how I had been treated and understood things were difficult. She was a breath of fresh air and work became a pleasant place to be again. However, I was so glad when I received confirmation that I would be able to move to the response unit.

I had worked with the majority of this team before, so it was an easy transition. I enjoyed working with them, we had some good camaraderie, PC Nayar one of our colleagues mum used to make some amazing food for him to bring in to the team, he always said she wanted to make sure we were all fed well so we could do our job and how proud she was, it was a lovely thing for her to do and a police officer will seldom turn down free food especially when it's that good.

So, I was extremely shocked when in 2015 PC Nayar was arrested for cultivating a cannabis farm in a house he owned and accessing the police computer systems to help his crime syndicate and evade arrest. On searching his house police found £26,000 worth of cannabis growing along with hydroponic growing equipment, drug dealing paraphernalia and a large amount of cash. He was fired and found guilty at court and is currently in prison after receiving a four year sentence. Which isn't enough if you ask me? I often think of his mother and how devastated she would be.

I was even more shocked when another officer from this team had been arrested in 2018 on suspicion of police corruption, namely abusing his position as a police officer for a sexual purpose, it is reported he abused his position whilst running a cadet programme aimed at 13 to 17 years olds and is currently suspended from duty and on police bail whilst the independent office of police conduct investigates.

It disgusts me that these people are in a position of authority and should be setting a good example, yet use this position as power to commit crime and abuse not only the system, but the young and vulnerable within our society.

PRE-WEDDING ASSAULT

It was a few weeks before the wedding, I was at work when comms asked if I could go and collect one of our regular missing from home persons. I was with one of my colleagues Brian, I had dealt with this female numerous times before. She was a patient in the psychiatric hospital but is granted a few hours leave during the day, if she doesn't return, she is reported as missing. Having dealt with her before I knew she would be spending her time in the local pub.

We went straight to the pub, and as expected there she was at the pool table with three men having an alcoholic beverage. I approached the female and she immediately recognised me, she was in good spirits and asked if Brian and I would like to have a drink with her, we politely declined and she knew it was time for her to go back to the hospital, she asked me if she could finish her drink, she only had a little bit left, it wouldn't do any harm, so I sat next to her and we had a chat whilst she finished.

We notified the hospital we had located the female and to prepare for our arrival. A few minutes later she finished her drink stood up and said come on then, take me back. We had a giggle and walked back to the van. She jumped in the cage of the van, I closed the van doors. Brian was driving and I got in to the front passenger seat and we took the short drive to the hospital.

The female was very chatty and within five minutes we were parking up next to the unit the female was a patient in. I got out of the van and walked round to the rear doors and opened them, as I did the female came at me like a raging banshee, bringing her hands which were now clasped together down from over her head and hit me in the face like she was wielding a sword, my head flew backwards and hit the cage door with such force it flung the door backwards, as my head came back forwards once again she brought her hands down from above her head and smashed them into my face all whilst screaming I was too pretty for this earth and needed to die, with the second blow my head once again snapped backwards hitting the cage door and I fell to the ground.

I don't actually recall what happened for a short period, I just woke to the female on top of me kicking and punching me with my colleague Brian trying to restrain her, we managed to get the female off me, and Brian and I placed her on the ground, the commotion must have alerted the hospital staff as they appeared within seconds to help restrain the female and one of Doctors administered some medication to calm the female down.

I stood up and the pain in my face was excruciating, I could taste the blood running down to my mouth, I struggled to move my arm and my trousers were ripped showing a laceration and grazes to my knee and leg. I was in immense pain, when a male who had stood by and watched this take place, asked whilst smiling if I was ok.

I snapped back "Do I fucking look ok?" I immediately regretted my words and had let the situation get the better of me, I was covered in blood, in a lot of pain and the male had just stood by and watched this happen. I apologised profusely to the male who then joked;

"Ahh, it's ok, I'd have said much worse, well at least it happened in a hospital grounds hey" he laughed at his own joke as I laughed back.

He was right though, we were a short hobble from A&E where I attended for treatment. Upon seeing the doctor, he asked me if my nose had always been wonky, I nervously laughed whilst confirming it was not. He told me it looked broken as he mobilised something in my nose with a click,

. . .

"You are going to have two nice black eyes tomorrow" he said,

"Would you believe I have my hen do at the weekend a hair trial and my wedding are only weeks away" I replied.

"Well I hope your theme is black, that way the eyes will go well" he said,

"It is a black and white colour scheme" I replied and we both laughed, though I think mine was more a nervous laugh and if I didn't laugh, I think I may have cried.

The Doctor told me to have a follow-up appointment for my nose once all the swelling had gone down to see if surgery was required. I left the hospital that night with my arm in a sling I had ligament and tendon damage, I was unable to walk properly because of ligament and tendon damage as well as swelling and grazing to my leg, a bust lip, concussion, two already developing black eyes and a new swollen and wonky nose! It was only a few weeks until my wedding. Great I thought, just another way this job impacts on my life.

I didn't even want a hen do, but I went to mine with a limp, black eyes (though happily they were fading), my arm still in pain and I was unable to cut my food and couldn't drink any alcohol because of my medication.

I went back to the follow-up appointment and it seemed my nose had healed itself, although I had reported loss of smell and severe headaches so referred to the ENT specialist for further investigation.

DATA PROTECTION BREACH

The day had finally arrived, Friday 1st October 2010, the day I will become Mrs Hill. To my relief the visible injuries I had sustained had healed.

Michelle one of my closest friends and bridesmaids had come to Rookery Hall the night before with me as I wanted to have a relaxed morning and get ready at the venue. I had been awake since 3am, I was calm, excited and I was full of mixed emotions, it wasn't going to be the wedding I envisioned as a child as I wasn't going to have a single family member at my wedding, it also wasn't going to be the wedding I actually wanted but I was marrying the man I loved and that was all that mattered.

I made myself a cup of tea and sat listening to the rain pounding on the widows, I sat on my huge four poster bed and felt something I wasn't expecting to feel, lonely.

. . .

I was expecting Michelle to knock at 8am so we could go and enjoy breakfast at our leisure before the makeup artist and hair stylist arrived. Like clockwork there was a knock at my door at 8am, I was showered and in my robe, ready for a relaxed breakfast. I opened the door and Michelle excitedly greeted me giving me a hug and saying happy wedding day and it was just what I needed, I held back the tears that I felt coming, but to feel genuine love from Michelle on my special day made me realise I did have family at my wedding.

The makeup artist and hair stylist arrived at my room and my other bridesmaid Alice arrived too. The photographer came shortly after. We were having a lovely time when Jack's mum and sister turned up, they were also getting their hair and makeup done by the makeup artist. As soon as they entered the room the atmosphere changed. When they came in Sue said happy wedding day, but Jane just said hello and didn't acknowledge the fact it was my wedding day. My dress was hanging up on the bed and the best comment Jane could muster was it was nice.

Michelle and Alice already had their makeup done and I was next, I wanted to look natural and have my hair pinned back up in timeless barrel curls. I opened a bottle of champagne and decided to enjoy the moment for what it was, my wedding day.

. . .

My friends were obviously aware of the relationship I had with Jack's family and were being nice and polite with Sue and Jane, including them in the conversations and making sure they were topped up with champagne.

There was another knock at the door and it was Anita, my best friend since I was three and her mum Auntie Anita. They were the closest to actual family I had at my wedding. Anita was so excited and almost started crying when she saw me, Auntie Anita's eyes filled with tears when she saw me too and couldn't manage to get any words out for a few minutes and had to sit down. It was the reaction I always envisaged a mother or father would have when they saw their daughter getting ready on their wedding day, so I felt incredibly special that I had such a reaction from her.

It was time for me to get my dress on, and we were all set, I felt incredibly beautiful. Unfortunately, the weather wasn't on my side and it was raining, so we have some lovely photographs of the master of ceremony helping me hold my wedding dress to keep it off the ground, whilst my bridesmaids and Julian were keeping us dry with some hotel umbrella's for the short walk to the ceremony room.

This was it, the moment I had been waiting for, I was about to walk down the aisle and marry the man I loved. My bridesmaids stood in front of me waiting for the doors to open, they looked absolutely stunning and I linked arms with Julian, my closest male friend and Michelle's soon to be husband was walking me down the aisle, he looked very handsome in his Scottish Kilt.

Then I heard the master of ceremony announce my arrival and the doors opened to the beautiful sound of the harp playing Pachelbel Canon in D major.

My eyes immediately filled with tears as I could see Jack stood at the end of the aisle looking handsome in his grey three piece suit.

Julian squeezed my arm and laughed saying "Are you sure you want to do this?" and with that we both laughed and started to walk down the aisle.

The room looked beautiful and elegant just as I had imagined, as I approached Jack, he had a huge smile on his face and tears in his eyes. I kissed Julian on the cheek and gave Michelle my bouquet to hold and with that I took hold of Jacks hands and he kissed me and told me I looked beautiful.

The female registrar told us all to sit to sit and welcomed everyone. She then said;

"Helen has done a wonderful job and planning this beautiful

day, but the one thing Helen couldn't control was the weather and unfortunately today the rain doesn't seem to want to stop, though I have been told a wet bride is a happy bride"

And with that the whole room burst out laughing and any nerves or tension were gone.

The ceremony was a relaxed one, with beautiful readings from Anita and Philip, Jack's Dad.

Then we were announced as husband and wife and I signed my name for the first time as Hill.

We didn't have much time between the ceremony and the wedding breakfast to take photographs as we started the ceremony thirty minutes later than planned whilst waiting for Jack's Auntie and Uncle, but I was ready to eat as I was starving.

The wedding breakfast was absolutely delicious,

In between the wedding breakfast and the evening reception I didn't want guests to get bored so I hired some casino tables to keep guests entertained during the changeover period, I'm also not a big fan of dancing so I wanted something as part of the evening entertainment so guests could have an alternative option and it went down a storm, not one seat was vacant the whole time.

I'm also someone who finds the small things are just as important as the big things and sometimes more memorable, so next to the guest book I had a little sweet station, I had Yankee candle's around the venue to create a wonderful smell, I had a lovely photograph of Jack and I in a frame that guests could write wishes and messages on for us, to name a few so when I was stopped by one of Jane's friends and told it was the most thoughtful and elegant wedding they had ever been to it meant a lot to me. What I wasn't expecting was the reaction that lovely comment got from Jane, I didn't realise she was stood next to us.

"Oh no it isn't our Sue's was" she snarled and with that she walked away. I was speechless, I didn't know what to say so decided to ignore her comment and thanked her friend for his kind comment.

The reception started and more people were arriving, I was nervous for the first dance so I had a little bit more champagne than I normally would to calm my nerves, I unlike Jack don't enjoy being the centre of attention so when it was time for the first dance, I was a little tipsy and enjoyed dancing.

. . .

The reception was in full swing and though we had heard the band play before they were absolutely fantastic and you couldn't get me off the dance floor.

Anita later told me her and Auntie Anita couldn't stop laughing as one of the main reasons I hired the casino tables was because I didn't enjoy dancing, yet I didn't sit at the casino tables all evening as I was too busy throwing some shapes on the dance floor.

I was having a fantastic evening, but it was getting quite late and people were slowly but surely starting to leave, when Jane came over to me and grabbed hold of my arm;

"I never wanted you to marry my son, I've never liked you and never will, you aren't good enough for my son, but I can't do anything about it now" she scowled.

I was absolutely gob smacked, I couldn't believe she would stoop so low as to accost me on my wedding day, I had tears running down my cheeks yet still she wouldn't stop saying horrible things about me.

Philip, Jack's Dad came over took hold of Jane's arm and kept saying, "Come on Jane, that's enough".

. . .

But Jane was relentless, I'm not one who doesn't stand up for myself, but this was my wedding and out of respect for Jack I held back. One of Jane's best friends and her daughter came over and took me away to the sofa and sat with me whilst I wiped the tears from my face.

They told me Jane had had too much to drink and I should ignore her, that I was the best thing that had ever happened to Jack and they could see how happy he was with me. Her daughter was just as kind with her words and with their reassurance I put the incident to the back of my mind not wanting it to cloud the rest of the evening, I didn't want to give Jane the satisfaction of ruining my wedding day.

I went over to Jack and told him what had happened, and he told me to just ignore her and forget about it.

As the night continued and more people began to leave, I was exhausted and no longer in the party mood so I asked Jack to come to bed with me it was past 1am, he stated he wanted to stay down and party with his friends and with that I walked off back to the bridal suite on my own, not telling anyone I was leaving.

When I got to our room, I had the arduous task of getting myself out of my wedding dress and taking the incredible amount of hair pins out of my hair it must have taken me about 45 minutes but once out I fell into the bed and I must have been asleep within seconds.

I didn't hear Jack come to bed but he was up early and woke me as he was clattering around getting ready, I asked what he was doing as he said he was going to have breakfast with his friends, I couldn't believe what I heard, it's our first morning as husband and wife and he wanted to enjoy breakfast with his friends. I told him to wait for me get to ready and we went downstairs together to have breakfast with our guests who'd stayed over at the hotel.

We were having a small garden party and barbecue later in the day at Jack's parent's house, though after Jane's performance last night I didn't feel like going, it was after all to celebrate our wedding, so I had to go.

We were all in the garden and it was nice to hear everyone talking about the wedding and how much they enjoyed it.

I got up out of my chair to go inside and get a drink when I overheard a conversation about my dress, they were discussing how beautiful it was and one of the nicest dresses they had seen when I heard Jane snarl.

"Oh no, our Sue's was much nicer".

. . .

I really wanted to say something to her about her whole behaviour at this point but instead decided against it, I ignored her comment and continued in to the kitchen to get a drink.

As I stood there pouring my drink, I looked out of the kitchen window into the garden and I looked at Jane, it was just over 24 hours since I married Jack and I should have been incredibly happy but I couldn't help but think, what had I done marrying into this family, she is a horrible nasty woman and now she would be round for the rest of my life, then I looked over and saw Jack and the amount of love I had for this man made all the negative thoughts leave my mind, he was the reason. A few hours later we said our goodbyes as we were up early the following day to go on our three week honeymoon, Florida and a Caribbean cruise, I couldn't wait.

A few weeks after our return from our honeymoon I discovered I was pregnant. I was elated.

Though we agreed to start trying for a baby once we were married, I couldn't believe we were pregnant so soon, I couldn't wait to tell Jack.

He was on night shifts, so he was sleeping, I decided I wanted to make a lovely meal then tell him the exciting news over dinner. It was just after 6pm and I couldn't contain myself for much longer so as dinner was nearly ready, I ran upstairs and woke Jack, I told him I was cooking dinner and for him to come down shortly.

"I want more sleep" he replied, "It's only 30 minutes earlier, could you get ready and come down I'd like to talk to you and I'm making dinner" I said.

"No, I want more sleep" he snapped, "Come on Jack, you've been in bed practically all day, I just want to talk to you" I said enthusiastically.

"What is it?" he snapped. He started to become angry with me and I was quickly losing the excitement of telling him the news.

"I don't want to tell you like this" I said "Just get ready and come down dinner will be ready in ten minutes".

"Just fucking tell me Helen, now you've woke me" he snapped.

"I'm pregnant" I snapped back as I started to walk out of our bedroom and back downstairs;

. . .

"Oh great" he replied sounding disappointed? My heart sank and tears filled my eyes as I walked downstairs.

I went into the kitchen and plated up dinner expecting Jack to come and join me, though it was a further forty minutes before he appeared.

I was sat on the sofa when Jack came down dressed and ready for work, he walked passed me without looking at me and into the kitchen, when he came out again, he said he was going to work, I couldn't believe he was behaving like this.

"Do you not want to talk about it?" I asked, "No, I'm going to work", he responded without even looking at me.

"What's wrong?" I asked. And with that we began to argue about me being pregnant so soon and Jack walked out saying he didn't want to talk about it.

I never imagined telling Jack the happy news would go like this, this is what we discussed, getting married and having a family.

A few days after we discovered I was pregnant we went to

tell his parents the news, I was like a bubble fit to burst, I wanted to tell everyone.

We were sat at the kitchen table with Jane, and Philip was in the living room, I went and asked Philip to come in to the kitchen as we wanted to talk to them, I asked them what they were doing in July/August of next year and they asked why?

"You're going to be grandparents" I said excitedly.

"You're pregnant?" said Philip with a smile on his face.

"We're already grandparents" said Jane.

"Yes, we're having a baby" I said, choosing to ignore Jane's comment.

From the moment I found out I was pregnant I was in love with my baby, I knew I was put on this earth to be a mother and I had so much love to give I couldn't wait to hold my bundle of joy in my arms.

When I returned to work I was placed in the public service team, due to being pregnant, it was the same group of people I had previously worked with, so I was happy to be in there. They were a good team and good police officers so I enjoyed my days at work again.

The days began to fly by, and I was already half way through my pregnancy when I received an email from Chief Inspector (CI) Pew asking me to go to his office as he needed to see me.

Things had been going so well in the public service team, so I was surprised to receive an email of such nature, I automatically thought I was in trouble for something. I had never had any dealings with chief inspector Pew before so I didn't know what to expect.

I went his office straight away, it was a typical oversized Chief Inspectors office with a large round table with enough seats for six people at the front of the office, numerous book cases and filing cabinets scattered around and a large desk towards the rear of the office where Inspector Pew was sat, I knocked on the door and CI Pew looked up at the door.

"Can I help you" he said with a stern look on his face, "Helen, you sent me and email asking to see me", "Yes, come in" he said. I walked in to his office as he picked up a file off his desk to the left of him.

. . .

He informed me it had been brought to his attention about my brother, he had a file that he wanted me to take a look at, he wanted me to write a statement of my relationship with him, any contact I have with him and any contact details I have for him and bring it back CI Pew.

"I don't have any relationship with my brother, and I haven't had contact with him for years, so I don't have much if anything to offer" I said.

"Well just write what you do have, your relationship, last contact and we'll go from there" he said.

"Why am I being asked to do this?" I asked curiously.

He told me they were asking every officer who has a relation known to police to provide details of their relationships and contact for transparency, especially the ones who are currently wanted by police.

"Sure, I can understand that, I'll get it back to you this week" I replied.

He nodded and I turned and left the room. As I was walking back to my office, I couldn't help but think how dare my brother put me in such a position, he knew I was a police officer but people like him don't care about others, that how he is in this situation in the first place.

I got to my office sat down at my desk, luckily it was at the back of the office with the computer screen facing the wall, the last thing I wanted was people knowing why and what I was doing.

I opened the file and I was in complete shock, there right in front of me were all the details of my brothers' heinous offences, every little horrifying detail including his victims' details. Victims' names, addresses, schools and telephone numbers, not only did it have the victim's details, but any witnesses involved also.

I closed the file and quickly walked back up to the CI's office, as fast as my pregnant body would allow me to waddle, my heart was pounding, I was furious and angry that I had been given all of his details. I got to the CI's office and knocked on his door.

"Hello again" I said, "I think you may have given me the wrong file".

"Jack Davis is your brother" he replied, with a confused expression on his face.

. . .

"Yes, unfortunately he is, but this file contains every single detail of his crimes right down to his victims' details, contact numbers and home addresses" I said also confused.

"Yes, just get that report I asked for back to me this week" he replied.

"I will but this is a data protection issue, I am the offender's sister, I shouldn't have access to this information" I said worryingly.

"Its fine, just get me the information I've asked for" he snapped waving his hand to dismiss me.

I couldn't believe that I had been given this information, it was a clear breach of data protection as I had no right to have to have this knowledge. It made me wonder what other information is given to officers relating to family members involved in crime.

These victims expect the police to keep them safe and only give their information to the people who require it. Not all police officers uphold the law and if given the wrong person who knows if they would take matters in to their own hands in order to protect their family member. Luckily for my brothers' victims, I am not one of those officers.

. . .

I went back to my office and confided in a colleague, she was as shocked as I was and advised me to complete the requested report and get all of the information handed back to the chief inspector as quickly as possible. I did the report and with all the details of our relationship including any contact information I had for him, I didn't feel the slightest bit guilty handing over any contact information I had for my brother.

To me he was a disgrace and deserved to be in prison and away from anyone he could cause harm to. I went to CI Pew's office and knocked on the door, he was sat at his desk on the telephone, and motioned me to wait by mouthing "One minute" raising his finger.

I waited at the door like I was waiting outside the head mistress's office. He finished his call and shouted for me to come in.

"Here is the report on my brother you asked for and here is the file you gave me" I said as I handed him the report.

"If you have any future contact with your brother you need to submit a further report outlining all the details" he replied,

. . .

"That's only if he is wanted for a crime though I'm sure?" I asked confused.

"No, any further contact on your brother" he said matter of fact, "Why?" I asked.

"Because I am your Chief inspector and I am asking for the information and you are a police officer and any information you have is to be reported!" He snapped

"Just because I am a police officer doesn't mean I have to declare all information in relation to my brother if he isn't wanted for a crime, if he is wanted for a crime and I have information I will happily do so however if he is not, you cannot use my position to obtain and supply information on my brother." I said standing my ground.

How dare he think I would happily keep the police updated with intelligence on an offender just because they were a relation this isn't ethical.

"If I ask you to report future information on your brother, you will do so, do you understand?" He snapped angrily.

Yet again, I had encountered another police officer who didn't like their power to be challenged.

. . .

"As I said if he is wanted, I will never hold back any information that will aid in his arrest. However as he is not currently a suspect, I will not provide any information I have, just to keep police intelligence updated: not that I have contact with him anyway." I retorted.

"You don't make things easy on yourself Helen" He replied.

"Are we done now Inspector Pew?" I asked. As I have no respect for the man it did not cross my mind to call him 'Sir'.

"We're done" he said,

I turned and left the office.

SEX DISCRIMINATION

My pregnancy was stressful because of the miscarriages, I was constantly nervous about losing this precious baby too. We were under a consultant at the hospital, so I was having bi-weekly check-ups, and all was going well. However, I was suffering with sever pain in my pelvis which turned out to be symphysis pubis dysfunction. I could barely walk so when I was told by supervision I was a liability for health and safety reasons to be at work I was only too happy to take the extra time off work prior to the arrival of our baby. I spent the remaining weeks before our baby's arrival at home resting whilst also preparing for this incredible, life changing event.

On August 9th, 2011 after traumatic labour we welcomed our beautiful baby girl Nova to the world. I had never felt so much love, she was perfect. Unfortunately, after just a few hours it was evident she was poorly, she was a radioactive yellow colour and the look of concern on the nurse's face when she came for our checkup, said it all.

The paediatrician told me they needed to take her to the neonatal unit and needed to run some urgent tests. We were told they would come and get us in a short while, however after nearly 12 hours, we were still unable to see our daughter. We were constantly asking for updates so, when we were told that our daughter had a rare blood condition and we were to prepare for the worse our hearts dropped.

They were preparing her for a blood transfusion, had performed a lumbar puncture on her as she was also showing signs of Meningitis or Sepsis. My world began to crumble. When we were finally allowed to visit our little daughter it suddenly became real our baby was in an incubator (that only had a small peep hole for us to see her from and no way to touch her) smothered in aluminium foil which was illuminated blue from the UV lights.

There were tubes coming from every part of her little body and she had tiny goggles on her to protect her eyes from UV damage. No one wants to see their baby in such a devastating situation. After four long days I could finally touch my baby girl, though she had to stay in the neonatal unit for almost two weeks, I was elated to at last bring her home. During this time, I would wonder if she would be on the got to go home wall or the in remembrance wall, so it was an incredible feeling to see our photograph on the got to go home wall.

It was wonderful to finally be a mother, for the first time in my life I felt unconditional love, being a mummy was a job I knew I was born to do but bloody hell, it's the most exhausting one in the world. Jack wasn't very supportive, moaned if I asked him to change a nappy or allow me to have a sleep in. I was breast feeding so couldn't share the feeding duties at first but when we moved to expressing, he moaned if I asked him to feed our daughter whilst I got some sleep. It got so bad I didn't ask him to help anymore. Our relationship was becoming strained, I was exhausted both physically and emotionally.

It was fast approaching our friends Michelle and Julian's wedding and I had the honour of being a bridesmaid. Michelle's hen do was a weekend in London and I was really looking forward to it. However, leading up to it I had constant comments about me not going because Jack would have to look after the baby and its safe to say he wasn't happy about this nor prepared to handle a baby he had barely learnt to care for.

He told me I was too fat to wear the burlesque outfit and although I had not yet lost all the baby weight I was only a UK size 12. Slowly but surely, he was hacking away at my confidence with his negative comments in tow with constantly making me worry about leaving him alone with the baby for a whole weekend. So, before I knew it, I had made up an excuse not to go on the hen do. I couldn't tell

Michelle the truth and I was gutted I didn't go, though I can assure you Jack went on the lad's weekend away for Julian's stag do.

It was almost time for me to go back to work following my maternity leave, so I had to start the process of asking for a flexible shift pattern, I thought this would be a straightforward process, as the force appeared to be supportive towards women with family responsibilities. There were numerous female officers working Monday to Friday day shifts and a variety of other flexible working shift patterns, and most had a better support system in place than my husband and me.

The only child care assistance we would have was a fantastic nursery in our home town. The owners had the incredible foresight to accommodate parents who work various shifts and allowed those parents a flexible system during the hours of 07:30 and 18:00. We were fortunate enough to find this place. When we went for our tour around the nursery, I felt my heart sink. The place was lovely the children were clearly happy and enjoying their time there, which was comforting, but I never imagined it would be this hard to leave my daughter and return to work. With that sinking feeling in my heart, I could not help but shed some tears at the thought.

I submitted my request asking to work day shifts from Monday to Friday, as I could easily arrange child care during those hours it was the most convenient plan for both me and my baby. I didn't see this being a problem as many other female officers with children had these hours implemented prior to me going on maternity leave. Following my submission, I received an email inviting me for a meeting in June 2012 to discuss my application for flexible working with Chief Inspector Pew, the same CI I challenged 18 months previously concerning his breach of data protection relating to my brother's criminal records. I was incredibly nervous about this meeting but thought it would be a formality in arranging my return.

I knocked on the open door of Chief Inspector Pew's office and he invited me in. It was the same office I had been called into for the Data Protection incident. I took Nova along with me, which also broke the ice a little. CI Pew invited me to sit at the round table and explained that the purpose of the meeting was to find a mutually agreeable, flexible working pattern for my return to work, as he would not permit what I had requested. He then explained that as with all flexible working request, these would have to be presented to the senior leadership team during their weekly meeting for discussion and resolution of any divisional matters.

He told me that when it was mentioned that I had submitted a report asking for Monday through Friday day shifts the senior leader ship team simply laughed at my request. He said they thought it was 'hilarious' and ridiculed me for my request. I thought this displayed a considerable lack of discretion and professionalism, and suspected that there was an element of schadenfreude within his words. I found these comments to be very insulting to say the least. He informed me that during my maternity leave the force was having a restructure and upon my return they would be implementing a new four week shift pattern named PMIT.

I tried to explain to CI Pew the difficulties I had with childcare, that outside nursery hours of 07:30 to 18:00 I had no one to take care of my daughter except myself and husband who is also a police officer on a five week shift pattern and in a specialist department, so the scope for flexibility with him was minimal.

His response to my legitimate request was to simply retort "That's not my problem". Sensing the negativity brewing in the discussion, I then informed CI Pew that as I was still breast feeding my daughter, I had to be present for feeding and not my husband. "Well, how long are you expecting to do that for?" He asked, rather disdainfully.

I was shocked that he would ask such a personal question in such a demeaning manner. I was extremely embarrassed but informed him as long as I am able to due to my daughter's health issues.

CI Pew's response to this was to inform me that the force would not accommodate this for such a long amount of time and I should express: I found this surprising, considering the numbers of female officers whose family commitments were accommodated for.

I tried to inform him that my daughter can't drink from a bottle, but he wasn't interested in listening to what I had to say, he interrupted me and said, "Helen, you are a woman who has just had a baby and trying to return to work full-time in a 24 hour emergency service. Unfortunately, you cannot have it all, you were aware of this before you had a baby."

I couldn't help but cry. He didn't want to assist in finding a mutually agreeable solution. Instead, he wanted me to act as their puppet and do as they told me to like I was a little child. Any suggestions I came up with were laughed off or immediately declined. The meeting concluded with nothing resolved and left me feeling like I couldn't return to work under such circumstances.

I felt the manner in which this meeting was dealt with was extremely unprofessional and was nothing short of sexual discrimination. He belittled me and made me feel even worse for wanting to return to work after having a baby. The irony was the Chief Constable of the police force was publicly stating the force wanted to assist new working mothers in returning to work and this meeting was anything but what the Chief Constable was promoting.

. . .

I was already stressed and suffering with anxiety due to the ongoing health problems that myself and my daughter were suffering from, along with problems within my marriage, I couldn't see a way forward with CI Pew. This compounded issues, causing me to have a panic attack.

I went to my doctor who signed me off on sick leave. I immediately reported to work that I was unfit for duty and within a few days, I received a telephone call from CI Pew.

He was extremely condescending and angry in his tone of speech he clearly had no concern for my welfare. He informed me that he was very unhappy with me, was angry that I had reported sick and it was a personal insult to him that I had done so.

He believed that I had not given him chance to accommodate me. I tried to reason and explain the situation, but CI Pew had no interest and wouldn't let me talk. The call ended with CI Pew questioning my career choice and commitment. His position was uncompromising, unconstructive and one of indignation; How dare an officer report unfit for duty, regardless of the supporting medical evidence. Despite the official line made by the force of being supportive of officers with families or health issues, I had experienced the polar opposite. It was just empty rhetoric. I had been belittled, ignored and had my integrity questioned for raising a legitimate request for support.

. . .

After weeks of stressful negotiations, which included being told to use my annual leave to cover child care and with minimal movement on the force's behalf, I was told I would be working a final draft of the shift pattern produced by CI Pew. This shift pattern would still force me to use annual leave to cover childcare and I felt as if deliberate pressure was being applied to make my position impossible.

During this process I was required to undergo a CT and MRI scan after suffering a head trauma received during an on duty assault. Unfortunately (or perhaps fortuitously) the scan also showed I had a tumour/mass in one of my maxillary sinuses and I was informed it would require surgery to remove the mass and test the findings. Because of the symptoms I was exhibiting they were worried about the diagnoses. I was scheduled for surgery in August and I informed CI Pew of this to which he unsympathetically responded,

"There is always something delaying your return Helen".

I later had the surgery and to my relief it was a benign tumour.

During this time I was informed by CI Pew that the force was not going to be implementing the new four week-shift pattern (known as PMIT) and we had to go back to the drawing board and begin working on a "flexible" working pattern that worked alongside the current nine week shift pattern and the previously agreed shift pattern. This created a great deal of uncertainty and stress for me, as nothing was being resolved. Once again CI Pew was not willing to allow much scope for flexibility, even suggesting I would have to go part time for the force to be able to accommodate me.

After weeks of negotiations and little movement on CI Pew's behalf and with the imminent prospect of being forced onto zero pay I had no other option but to return to work and accept a shift pattern that once again required me to use my annual leave to cover child care. I was stationed at Sandford South police station in the neighbourhood policing team.

Despite working an impossible shift pattern and having to use my annual leave allowance to cover child care I enjoyed working with the team at Sandford South. It was good to be back at a substation and not having the senior leadership team micro managing your activities. It was a really laid back and relaxed team, working with them was enjoyable. Sergeant Cole was an affable and approachable man, and a fair sergeant.

The substation was not without its own issues. However, one particular victim of crime, a resident of the affluent areas on the South of the division who had been an unfortunate victim of burglary, appeared to enjoy a very personal level of service from one particular officer. Although it is standard for a noticeable police presence at a crime scene for a few days, this became a regular occurrence for this one victim.

One of my colleagues, PC Stone, who was the beat officer for the area, was apparently receiving 'gifts' from this individual, in the form of a Rolex watch, hot air balloon rides, tickets to Premier League football matches and much more. There was no attempt to conceal this, he enjoyed the 'perks' he received as much as he enjoyed sharing his stories to the other officers. In fact, far from being alone in being a recipient of such generosity, the Neighbourhood Policing team actually received a vehicle donation from this person, although supposedly via the correct channels. It's quite amazing how rules can be manipulated, bent and broken as and when it suits the police force.

Around November 2012 I received an email informing me of my posting following a skills audit for the PMIT restructure.

The outcome of this was for me to remain based at Sandford South police station within the neighbourhood policing team, the role my skills matched with was a neighbourhood beat officer. The email also requested officers requiring flexibility to submit working patterns for the proposed PMIT shift plan which was to be reviewed by the senior leadership team.

. . .

Following previous discussions with Chief Inspector Pew, I already had a five week shift pattern agreed and ready for the implementation of the PMIT restructure, therefore this shift pattern was submitted and to my surprise I received an email informing me this pattern was not suitable and was subsequently declined. I was extremely frustrated that I was being forced to go through the whole process again. I came up with numerous shift patterns that were both suitable for my personal circumstances and considered the force's requirements and forwarded them to the senior leadership team for review. They were, however, personally refused by both CI Pew and Chief Superintendent Ley.

Following the rejection of these shift patterns, we were given the option to appeal if we felt this was necessary. I submitted my appeal outlining my circumstances for asking for a flexible working pattern and was granted an appeal hearing with Detective Chief Inspector Letch in January 2013. Naively I went into this meeting thinking DCI Letch would be more understanding and accommodating due to her being a female officer with children herself. I was sorely mistaken.

During this meeting I again submitted the previously agreed shift pattern, which DCI Letch rejected, stating that as it was a five week pattern, I would be out of sync with my team at the start of week five. She proceeded to scribble over my requested pattern. DCI Letch stated that a five week pattern would be suitable for a move to response and gave me a mere seven days to formulate an amended rota. I knew of vacancies in the Prisoner Processing unit and the five week plan I suggested was suitable for transfer to this unit. Upon presenting this suggestion, I was told that this would not be suitable and was rejected immediately. I pressed for an explanation, but DCI Letch refused to provide any reasoning, simply repeating the vague justification that I 'wasn't suitable'. She stated I go away and come back with a shift pattern where I was with my team for more than 75% of the time.

It was evident that the outcome was a foregone conclusion regardless of what suggestions I offered. At the meetings conclusion, I was left facing the position of having to compare the response unit shift pattern to that of my husbands as my efforts to find an amicable solution had been continuously kiboshed by hostile management. It was at this point that I considered the option of submitting a grievance.

During this time the pressures of my home-life were mounting. My relationship with my husband had changed since our daughter's arrival. There was a dearth of physical support from him. This was tolerable whilst he was working.

What wasn't tolerable was the escalating amount of emotional abuse I received. This ranged from blaming me for becoming a mother and creating the situation with the force, calling me fat and denigrating my appearance, to telling me that he would take no financial responsibility for our daughter. Jack was never an enthusiastic father, often directing resentment toward me for blunting his extravagant lifestyle.

This wasn't accurate, as he still enjoyed his selfish pursuits (nights out with 'the lads', golfing trips abroad, lavish spending on clothes etc). If anything, it was my freedom that was pruned. I stopped going to the gym as Jack was incapable of coping with his child and would moan about the fact that he had to care for her. I was still carrying baby weight and found it difficult to shift without an outlet. I often had to endure him holding up photographs in front of me prior to pregnancy; "Where is she? Where is that hot woman I fell in love with? Look at the state of you." He would shout. "You're a mess, you're fat no one would want you now".

It was humiliating and demoralising, but I didn't have the energy or confidence to respond. Instead I would sit and cry. I didn't even want to get out of bed and if it wasn't for my daughter I wouldn't have. It was at this point that depression started to take a hold.

Whilst at work I noticed a vacancy for the CTU (Counter Terrorism Unit). This was a role that I had coveted for some time. Not only did the role offer a five week shift pattern, which would allow synchronising with my husbands, but they also offered flexible shift patterns. I approached my inspector (Insp. Bolton) who advised me to apply with his support. On the day the application was to be submitted, Inspector Bolton was not at the station and I couldn't contact him. I spoke to HR and they said I could submit the form and the Inspector could complete his supporting part upon his return.

The following week I received a response from HR to say I had passed the application stage which was the toughest stage and had been invited for an interview.

Upon the Inspectors return, I made a request for his written support for my application. I informed him that HR had already been in contact, notifying me that my sickness was acceptable and that they were happy to submit my application upon receiving Inspector Bolton's supporting statement. The grievance I had raised after my discussion with DCI Letch had been submitted a few days earlier.

I had been preparing hard for the role but just a few days before my interview, I received an email from HR, informing me that they had been contacted by DCI Letch (the same DCI who had prompted my grievance submittal). I immediately contacted HR, to be told that DCI Letch had contacted them demanding all the documentation I had submitted, as well as a copy of the CTU shift pattern. Presumably, this was in relation to my request for flexible working. They also relayed that DCI Letch had told HR that she was my line manager, and that she would not support my application, and that as a consequence, my application was terminated. Frustratingly, despite my circumstances, there was nothing they could do to counter this action.

I raised this matter with my Sergeant at the time. I was told by Sergeant Cole that Inspector Bolton had contacted him and told him to notify me that the senior leadership team would not support my application. When I pressed him for more information, I was told that no explanation for this decision had been given. I continued to seek an explanation for the refusal of support but was either stonewalled or couldn't be provided an answer by an understanding HR department.

With no valid, constructive explanation forthcoming, it was dawning on me that there was a concerted effort amongst the senior management to stifle my career at best or push me toward the door by making my position impossible. As a result, I raised this as part of my grievance, as I considered it to be a bullying tactic, when I finally got a response, I was informed I wasn't eligible to apply and the reason SLT did not support my application was because of my sickness record. I challenged this as I knew my sickness record wasn't an issue as I already had this confirmed with HR prior to submitting my application. Following this I was informed that it was an "oversight" and a "misunderstanding" and I was eligible to apply for the role and my application should have been supported.

. . .

To make amends, I was told I could apply for another CTU posting that had recently been advertised with their full support, although neither the role nor shift pattern I had wanted was being offered, I applied anyway. Despite their supportive words, I suspected they were gaslighting me and didn't truly believe I would be supported. Unsurprisingly, I failed to get past the application process, despite previous success. Although I was disappointed, I now felt a sense of vindication in my belief that I was the focus of a campaign of bullying.

At the next meeting with DCI Letch I asked her if she would take a look at a shift pattern that I had previously submitted that was based around the INPT pattern. I explained that although this may be a 20 week pattern, it provides over 80% working with my team and over 80% being present for my teams start of shifts. As with previous solutions I proposed, they were deemed 'unacceptable' with no clear rationale. I insisted that she take a look at it, as it provided the prerequisite good percentages she required.

Her response to my proposal was to claim I would not have a high enough percentage of parading with my team, giving the example that if I started at 0700hrs and the team started at 1200hrs I wouldn't be parading with my team. I tried to explain that I would be present for the 1200 parade and DCI Letch stated parading with my team means parading together and working the shift together and therefore my pattern was not acceptable. Again, as before, she began to frantically scribble through my shift proposals. It was apparent that every time I met the requirements, the goalposts were moved so as to ensure refusal.

She then asked for the response shift patterns, as discussed in my original appeal hearing with her. I provided her with three patterns for team D, E and B. I gave her the better pattern first, but as she looked over them one by one, the familiar pattern of frantic scribbling and rejection on the grounds of being 'unacceptable' surfaced again.

Upon rejecting the final pattern, she brusquely demanded the patterns for the other two shifts. I explained that, as these other two shifts were wholly incompatible with my family responsibilities, I had not completed the patterns for these shifts. I would not even be able to have a rest day with my family.

DCI Letch suggested that I should use my annual leave to spend time with my family, not at all conducive to providing an adequate work/life balance. When I put this to her, her tact changed, and suggested I take unpaid days off work to spend time with my family. She then stated that she wanted me to return the following week with shift patterns for Team A and C the two shift patterns that would give me no work life balance and not a single day off with my family. I informed her that I considered her behaviour to be bullying and that it was clear she was trying to coerce me into an unworkable position.

. . .

"Maybe you should go part time" she snapped back angrily as she pointed to the door and told me I had seven days to get back to her. I turned on my heel and left.

They neither wanted to compromise or assist me in finding an equitable solution, given the size of the force, there were ample units where not only could they accommodate a Monday to Friday daytime position, but they could also accommodate a flexible shift pattern that takes into consideration any health and work life balance issues, whilst also adhering to the requirements of the force and division. It was a simple fact of they wanted what they wanted and were not going to budge.

Shortly after this meeting I received a telephone call from DCI Letch making changes to the D teams' pattern and told me to consider them for the next meeting.

At the meeting with DCI Letch seven days later, I had prepared, as was requested, flexible shift patterns for A and C team and the two unsuitable patterns she demanded I do again. It was of little surprise that she found them unacceptable as I had changed rest days to allow some family time and she proceeded to scribble across them.

DCI Letch then referred to the twenty week pattern saying she had liaised with the Chief Inspector and they found it to be unacceptable as nearly 30% of the afternoon shifts had been deviated. Once again moving the parameters that were originally set out for me.

She then got the D team pattern out and we went through this. When she highlighted the changes she had made, I informed her that if I was to work from Sandford North it would take me an hour to get home and finishing a shift at 7pm gives me no room for being delayed either at work or during my journey home.

My husband had to leave for work at 8pm. If I was to be delayed, this would impact his ability to start on time. DCI Letch stated she had given me ample time to get home and that I would only be kept late in exceptional circumstances. She was more than aware that as a response officer you seldom finish your shift at the scheduled time. She refused to deviate the shift to allow me more scope for flexibility even by fifteen to thirty minutes. Even asking me for my post code so she could go on to her computer to check distance and travel time between work and home for both myself and husband.

There were so many problems with this shift pattern, there would be times I would finish at two or three am and get home an hour later and go to bed, my husband would then leave for work at five am and my daughter would then wake at six am only giving me two hours sleep if I was lucky. This would be for four consecutive nights causing me major sleep deprivation, which paired with a ten hour shift driving a police vehicle was a recipe for disaster but, she clearly did not care, she replied that was an issue I had to sort out with my husband.

There was one day where I was scheduled to begin work at 7 am when my husband was already in work finishing a night shift at 7am.Additionally, the nursery didn't open until 07:30am which meant as a result, I would not be able to get in to work until at least 9am.

It didn't matter how much I pleaded my case, my difficulties were simply dismissed.

DCI Letch stated that the force had to give officers twenty-eight days' notice before they can make an officer change a shift pattern, and that I had until 12:00 to reach a decision. When I explained I needed to speak to my federation rep and my husband, she reiterated I had until the end of the day as today is the twenty-eighth day until March 12th when PMIT is to be implemented and if I delayed my decision then there would be insufficient time to amend the shift pattern.

This meeting concluded with DCI Letch stating that I needed to get back to her by the end of the day with a decision and my two options are to stay at Sandford South and work the four week pattern as it is or move to Sandford

North on response and work the D team shift pattern with her amendments.

A couple of hours later I received a voicemail requesting an update regarding my decision.

I therefore sought advice from my federation rep and spoke with my husband and emailed DCI Letch. The email read as:

Ma'am,

Following our meeting today I feel like I have no other option as I have been pressured, bullied and intimidated into accepting a shift pattern that is the lesser of two evils. I will therefore be forced to work the D relief shift pattern with your uncompromising amendments.

I will point out I do not agree with your amendments, and your unwillingness to compromise will cause issues regarding, lateness, work life flexibility and child care arrangement for my daughter.

Regards

Helen

Throughout the meetings I had endured, I found DCI Letch

to be unreasonable with her proposals. I had found her to be brusque, aggressive and intimidating during the meetings and non-receptive to my circumstances or suggestions.

I felt bullied into accepting an unsuitable shift pattern, harassed with numerous phone calls putting pressure on me before the deadline had even past, intimidated with her actions and most of all I felt discriminated against for being a female officer with a young family trying to work a full time job within the force, who is only asking for flexibility, the very same things we practice against being Police Officers.

The irony of the whole process with DCI Letch was the fact that she herself had just had a flexible working pattern accepted to accommodate her child care circumstances but had absolutely no empathy or willingness to compromise for a female officer in the same circumstances.

POLICE BULLYING

I started on D relief, there were a lot of new faces on the team, but I also encountered a few familiar ones, including my old tutor. He actually apologised to me for not understanding how bullied I was by Sergeant Wall numerous years back, he told me she had been doing similar things with him and he realised I was in actual fact telling the truth back them. I didn't know if I was to be thankful or not, it wasn't because he had also been subjected to her bullying but it was because people had assumed I was a trouble maker, if a trouble maker is someone who stands up for themselves and other people being abused in various forms by police officers then yes, I guess I am a trouble maker and one I am proud to be.

The team were welcoming, they had different supervision than I had before, that's another problem with the police force, there is not much continuity.

. . .

I had my initial meeting to attend with the Sergeant May and Inspector Heaton, I take pride in being early so as always, I got to the inspector's office early, as I was approaching the room, I overheard Sergeant May and the inspector talking about me,

"I've never had any dealings with her, apparently she doesn't like taking orders" said May,

"Well, she'd better gets used to it otherwise things won't go well, she'll be here soon" replied the inspector.

I knocked on the door and entered, I already had my back up from overhearing their conversation. It wasn't really a meeting, it was them making sure I knew they were boss and I knew my place, very passive aggressive. I told them I wasn't happy with these circumstances but we will see how it goes and revaluate in a couple of months.

The first few shifts went ok, however before long it was the shifts where I would be home at 4am and up at 6am with our daughter. I was exhausted. I couldn't concentrate and wasn't fit to drive a police vehicle for 10 hrs, then it was the shift where I was scheduled to start at 7am but couldn't physically get to work until 9am.

I arrived at 9am and was immediately summoned to the

THE TRUTH BEHIND THE UNIFORM

inspector's office where both Inspector Heaton and Sgt May were waiting for me. They asked me why I was late, I told them I was not, and I had informed DCI Letch of my circumstances that caused me to be late but she would not amend the shift. They then began to reprimand me for being late, began to tell me my performance was lacking, and they had an action plan ready for me to sign, for being late and my lack of performance.

I refused to sign an action plan for being late and poor performance and they were well aware of the circumstances, I told them I was really struggling with the sleep deprivation, I was stressed and depressed and knowing when this shift would come around again, I would again be late I would be setting myself up to fail and having no support from supervision.

I asked them to refer me to occupational health. Sergeant May was not happy with me and had no empathy for my situation and told me he would not support me if I didn't sign the action plan, again I refused his blackmail tactic took the pen and action plan from him and scrawled "REFUSE TO SIGN" across it. They were not happy with me, telling me I would make things harder for myself and with that I left.

In 2018 Sergeant May, following promotion to inspector, was later arrested for murdering his police officer wife after leaving half way through his police shift , strangling the life out of her, breaking two bones in her neck, then proceeding to collect their children from school, laughing and joking with other parents while his dead wife's body was left in the boot of her car, and later dumping her body in a lake while their children slept unaware at home. Though not before trying to cover his tracks and sending texts to look like he believed she was still alive and playing the concerned husband. He was found guilty at court and later sentenced to a minimum of 19 years in prison.

A couple of weeks had passed by and I had not heard from occupational health, I was beginning to have panic attacks. I was receiving emotional abuse from my husband almost daily. At this point, I had a financial settlement come through for the injuries I had sustained just before my wedding. He took control of that money my money.

Although it was hardly my money anymore: I wasn't allowed to spend it due to him putting it into his savings account. Every time I tried to get a hold of the settlement money I was questioned as to what I was going to spend it on. Before I knew it, he had spent my settlement money on a new TV, a new suit, golfing equipment and he took a large amount of it to pay for his overdraft. He also had a couple of credit cards he was juggling and before long it was me who was told to take out a loan to consolidate his credit cards.

He refused to pay for any childcare, telling me again; I wanted her, so I can pay for her, that was the same for clothes and toys. He forgot to buy me gifts most of the time for birthdays and Mother's Day and I had to remind him many times the night before. He normally ended up online buying me gifts or saying he would take me shopping. It began to take its toll feeling neglected and forgotten about. Then he said he would take me on a family holiday for my 30th birthday, if I pay, he would pay me back. He never paid me back and I ended up paying for my own 30th birthday gift.

I told my husband I wanted to leave the police force; it wasn't good for our lifestyle but more importantly it wasn't good for my mental health. I was depressed. Uncaring, he told me when we got married I signed a contract and that contract was to continue to provide him with the same lifestyle we had then. I was not allowed to leave the police force unless I had a job that brought in the same amount of money if not more. I was devastated, could he not see my mental health was deteriorating? I was a mess… I couldn't continue this way, but it seemed money and materialistic things were more important to him than my health and our child. I was so stressed, depressed and exhausted I started hallucinating.

I was continuing with the grievance process but also consulted with a lawyer as I knew the force would never admit to anything and we started the process of taking the force to an employment tribunal.

. . .

Still, I had not heard anything regarding occupational heath despite being reassured they had submitted a referral. I contacted them, and they insisted they had never received a referral for me and unfortunately could not process me without a referral. I was furious. I headed straight to the Superintendent and told him my Sergeant and Inspector are lying about submitting a referral. He assured me he would look in to it and send an urgent referral himself. Days went by and still nothing, I contacted occupational health still they had received nothing. I was getting worse, I was struggling to cope.

I went to my Superintendent again who lied saying he had submitted a referral. He also asked me if I was recording my meetings with supervision as I seemed to recall them well, I didn't answer his question but knew someone had told them what I had done. By this point I felt like they were wanting me to fail, pushing me to the edge. Wanting, wishing something bad to happen to me. I had no support at work nor home; I was sinking deeper and deeper in to depression.

I went to submit some property in to the property store and there was a gun and ammunition, I just wanted to end this pain so I contemplated picking the gun up and ending it all when my phone rang and my daughters face popped up on the screen, it was my husband calling and with that came a moment a clarity, I burst out crying and had a panic attack. I went straight to the office and contacted occupational health informing them of what had happened. They made me an emergency appointment.

A few days later I was speaking with a colleague who informed me that there was a vacancy that had not been filled in their office for a long time. It was a Monday to Friday day time job, a role with hours I was told did not exist on the division, yet this post had been available the whole time I was requesting flexible working, it wasn't a glamorous job, it was with the coroner's office, however it fit with my requirements and once you have dealt with your first few dead bodies, you become used to them.

I went to speak with the superintendent in relation to this posting and he spat out some bullshit excuse for not offering me the post in the first place. I told him I wanted the position and would submit a report asking for that position and that I would be adding this in to my grievance and with that he said the position was mine and I would start the following week. It was a huge relief to know I would be working normal days shifts.

IMPOSSIBLE DECISIONS

I was stood there, not knowing what to say, thousands of thoughts racing through my head.

Did he really just say that? Did I hear him right? No, he wouldn't? Yes, he did! And in the blink of an eye my world fell apart.... I was given an impossible choice to make that would end my marriage either way.

It all started on a Friday morning in June 2013, when I received a call that would change my life. We were all packed ready for a weekend in Scotland as we were visiting our friends, Michelle and Julian, when I received a phone call from the Dr, I had recently had some routine blood tests done. However, the Dr congratulated me on my pregnancy and informed me I would need to book in for my early pregnancy assessment due to my previous pregnancy history. I was delighted but nervous as we hadn't planned this pregnancy.

I told my husband the wonderful news and I could tell immediately by the look on his face he wasn't happy, he told me he didn't want the baby and didn't want to talk about it, and I was not to tell anyone, my heart sank. He knew I wanted more children. I tried to talk with him.

"I don't want to fucking talk about it, I don't want the fucking baby" He shouted at me as he left the room.

We drove to our friends in Scotland as planned and spent the weekend with them, not once did we discuss the pregnancy and the weekend was a struggle both physically (as I was being sick) and emotionally (as I was devastated and in complete turmoil). I was desperate to speak with my friend, Michelle, but I knew I would get very upset and I didn't want to spoil the weekend.

Days went by. I tried to talk with him, but he would ignore me he didn't want to talk about it. We argued like never before and then one day, two weeks after the phone call, my world fell apart.

"I don't want the baby" he said, "I'm glad you lost the other babies, I never even wanted her" he said as he pointed to our beautiful 20 month old daughter Nova.

"I only married you and had her for you, if you have this baby our marriage is over. It's our marriage or the baby" and with that, he left.

My head was spinning, I couldn't stop the tears from streaming down my cheeks, did I really just hear my husband give me an ultimatum? No, I couldn't have. He wouldn't say that. Would he? Yes, he would. He did. My husband, the father of my precious daughter, the man I loved, was giving me an impossible choice. I had to choose between my family or a new life with the precious baby growing inside of me that would be a brother or sister for my daughter.

I felt like my heart had just been ripped out of my chest. How can I make this choice? How could he put me in this situation knowing how devastated the loss of my previous pregnancies had been to me?

For the next few days we barely spoke, when we did it was like WWIII, I had every conceivable possibility running through my head, I couldn't sleep, I binge ate, I was so consumed with trying to come to terms with what had happened and what to do. I didn't want to be a single mother to one child let alone two how would I cope? I didn't want to break my little family unit up even though it wasn't perfect, I didn't want my daughter to have a broken family. I also didn't want to break the wider family unit up, my in laws however dysfunctional they are, were the only family I had. I know the heartbreak of losing a baby that was so desperately wanted and here I was faced with making an impossible decision.

A few days later my daughter and I were then involved in a car accident that required an ambulance to attend, this unfortunately was on the area myself and husband police, I had to tell the paramedic of my pregnancy and in turn people at work found out.

My husband and I received congratulatory messages and calls from friends, could the situation get any worse I thought.

A few days later I came home from work, I took my daughter outside into our beautiful garden and watched her as she played with our dog in the glorious sunshine, oblivious to my heartbreak.

My husband came home. I asked him to come and sit with us and there I told him that I had made my choice, fighting back the tears I told him I had booked an appointment for the following day to terminate my pregnancy and save my marriage. He told me it was the right thing to do and he will tell people we suffered another unfortunate miscarriage.

As if the situation couldn't get any worse a friend put a congratulations message on Facebook, luckily, I saw it and removed the message, I told my husband and he was then concerned his family would see something and we had not told them. My husband phoned his mother and told her I was pregnant, but the baby is dying, and I needed to go to hospital the following day for assistance with the 'miscarriage'. I felt disgusting; I didn't want to do this. I desperately wanted my baby. I hated him

I didn't sleep that night, the next day was a blur, my husband dropped me at the hospital, and he went to our friend's house who were aware of the situation. I met with the Dr's and that day, I ended my pregnancy, I immediately regretted what I had done and right there in that moment I knew in my head marriage was over. I called in work sick that day.

My husband picked me up with my daughter, he gave me flowers and a 'thinking of you card'. What the fuck I thought, I felt sick.

I told him I couldn't look at him. I was devastated but I didn't have the energy for anything else.

. . .

THE TRUTH BEHIND THE UNIFORM

I tried to forgive him and continue with our marriage, but I fell into a deep dark depression. I couldn't leave the house. I hated myself for what I had just done. I hated my husband for giving me the devastating ultimatum that caused me to spiral so far into depression.

I wanted to sleep in separate rooms in the house whilst I dealt with destruction and grief my decision left me with. He continued to put me down: for gaining weight; for being in my PJ's all day; telling me I was a mess and constantly repeating why would anyone want to be with me.

He continued to put pictures of me looking beautiful and slim in front of my face and shout "Where is she? Why would I want you on my arm anymore? No one would want you" It was a daily struggle not to cry from the constant emotional abuse. I no longer wanted to feel the pain and hurt.

I was at rock bottom and the only light was my darling daughter. She kept me from ending it all because I couldn't bear to leave her and not see her and her smile again, to not hear her laugh again or to never hear the words "I love you mummy" made me cry. I couldn't leave her. I couldn't leave her with him and his family, who already treated her differently to her cousin because she was mine.

Things were so bad I went to see the Dr and was referred

for counselling and to see a psychiatrist. I was diagnosed with severe depression and started a course of medication.

I went back to work in the public service team with restricted hours and with Dr's advice along with the force medical practitioner, I would have to see them again before we made an increase in duties and hours, however after a few weeks my inspector called me into his office.

"Helen, you have been on restricted hours for a few weeks now, we need to increase them." He said.

"The Dr's said I need to see them before any hours are increased and I have an appointment with them next week" I said due to me barely sleeping, trying out new medication and suffering with side effects.

"I don't care what your Dr's have said, I am your inspector and you do as I say" he said, not liking me challenging his authority.

"There is a reason my Drs have given me restricted hours and they need to monitor me before I increase my hours" I said confused.

"I don't have to take into consideration what the Dr says, it's only advice, you will be increasing your hours from your next set of shifts and back to normal hours in a couple of weeks" he snapped clearly unconcerned for my health and wellbeing.

I went to the toilets and burst out crying. The Dr's didn't even want me back at work, I was only back at work because James was forcing me to keep bringing money into the house and it was destroying me. The force is supposed to have a duty of care and they didn't care about my health, they didn't take mental health seriously. I was just a number and my sickness statistics were making the division look bad. I couldn't do this anymore; this job is not worth my health and with that I went home and called in the next day as sick.

Because I had been on and off sick for a period of time the police decided to take me down the unsatisfactory performance route amounting to discipline and possible dismissal, I kid you not, despite me having a medical diagnosis instead of helping me get better they wanted to discipline and dismiss me.

I probably wouldn't have been so depressed if it wasn't for them, so with my Drs and lawyers advise I applied for ill health retirement alongside the process of taking the police to court with an employment tribunal for bullying, harassment and sex discrimination. I completed the form for ill health retirement which in turn, halted the unsatisfactory performance process. I poured my heart out into that form and explained everything I had been going through.

A few weeks after I submitted my ill health retirement form, my husband received a telephone call, he was at home on his rest day when my superintendent introduced himself to Jack. Jack put the call on loud speaker so I could overhear.

"I believe you are aware Helen has applied for ill health retirement?" he said to Jack.

"I am yes" Jack replied.

"Has Helen told you what she wrote on the form?" said Superintendent.

"I don't believe she has" said Jack.

"She has written about a time she wanted to kill herself at the police station" said superintendent.

"I didn't know that" said Jack.

"Well, because of this, we have concerns about Helen's

mental health, and we have concern for your daughter's safety and welfare and have therefore reported Helen to social services. We just wanted to inform you of this and that you will be contacted by social services" said the Superintendent.

I was furious and devastated: it was well over a year ago that I had that split second thought and they wouldn't help me at the time when I was practically begging to be referred to occupational health. They were more than aware I had sought professional help and was no longer in that frame of mind.

The fact that they would use something so personal with absolutely no reference to harm or negligence of my daughter against me just proved they had a vendetta against me and would try any tactic to discredit me and bully me into backing down with the employment tribunal, I was heartbroken.

Jack was furious with me, but I had absolutely no reason to tell Jack what I had put on the form, it was a confidential document and the Superintendent telling Jack was a clear breach of data protection.

He told me my depression was my own fault and he always knew I was a psycho and the diagnoses from the doctor just confirmed that I was crazy. I was exhausted. I had no fight left. My daughter was my world and I would never have done anything to hurt her, yet the police had such a campaign against me. Weeks went by and I never heard anything from social services which affirmed my belief regarding the personal vendetta against me and reassured me that social services believed I was not a risk to my daughter.

Then one day after my husband put me down again, my daughter saw me crying and began to cry herself and said, "Has Daddy made you cry again mummy?" and at that moment, my heart broke, my darling daughter who for the last few years had been witness to all of this. My depression, the way her Daddy was treating her mummy and my weakness for allowing him to do so. What kind of example was I setting for her? To be weak? To allow people to walk over her? To not stand up for herself?

Enough was enough! I was done. I couldn't wallow in myself pity any longer if not for my own sake for the sake of my daughter. She deserved better. I grew up in a hostile environment myself and due to this, I vowed never to do that to my own children and here I was allowing the same to happen. Well not anymore, I was petrified knowing what this meant, I was going to be a single mother.

So just after our daughters third birthday, I told my husband I wanted him to move out of our family home. It was extremely hard to do so, but I could never forgive him for the duress he put me under and the constant emotional abuse following my depression and pregnancy. He refused to move out and the arguments escalated.

He forced me to sell our beautiful family home threatening not to pay the mortgage, saying he would get me blacklisted for failing to pay. I couldn't afford it on my own as I was currently off work due to my depression and other medical issues. I told him that would make our daughter and I homeless and I would struggle to get a rental being off work sick, he didn't care and said, "Tough shit". He kept telling me that no one gets to dump him, and no one will want me. According to him, I was a psycho. I was scruffy. I was fat. I didn't care anymore and we accepted an offer on our house.

I had also been suffering with discharge from my right breast that I had left for so long that it had now turned black. I went to the Dr who immediately referred me for an urgent appointment at the hospital. I was seen immediately and told they needed to operate for a biopsy as he believed it could be ductal carcinoma in situ. I phoned Jack as I was worried and all he could say was hurry home because our daughter is doing his head in. I cried, I had just been given awful news and I was all on my own. I had no one to be there with me.

No one to support or help me through this. The following week, I went for my surgery. Upon recovery, the Dr told me they had to remove all of my ducts and some surrounding tissue as it was a lot worse than they initially thought. They did however believe they removed everything and I just had to wait for my results. Jack collected me from the hospital and said he was taking me to the solicitors to sign documents for selling the house. I had just come out of the hospital following my surgery and had been told I shouldn't sign any documentation for 48 hours and here was Jack threatening me with being homeless if I didn't go and sign the documents. I told him I was exhausted and hadn't even got the medical tapes off my arms and hands from the hospital there would be no way the solicitor would let me sign. He agreed and we went home, he would not relent, I signed documents the following day.

I spoke with the solicitor a few days later and advised her of the circumstances, she advised me she would not complete the sale until I had found somewhere to live with my daughter. I had just five days before we were due to complete the sale and I ended up finding the only property in the area that was suitable for us. Jack refused to take George ,our dog, as he was going to be living in his mums huge five bedroom house and she refused to have an animal there. So, I had to make sure George could be accommodated too, he was a rock throughout (animals really are family). I got him when we lost the first pregnancy so he was my way of coping and I wouldn't be without him.

My daughter and I moved into the rented accommodation it was horrible: it was mouldy and damp. Even though Jack was living with his mum and had minimal financial expenditure, at first, he refused child maintenance, he barely had our daughter either, preferred to go out partying and golfing instead. I was so broke, I struggled to put food on the table, I only heated my house when my daughter was home. I had to go to a local food bank to make sure we could have food over Christmas. I was devastated. How could this happen?

I was a police officer, yet they offered no support for my mental health or the poverty I was currently experiencing. I was selling things to pay bills. I was so embarrassed to tell anyone how bad things were that I hid myself away from everyone and only left the house when it was a necessity. I was so lonely. I tried to give things another go with Jack, but every time he left the house, I felt disgusted. Every time I would breakdown crying to one of my friends, Jo, she was a constant support during this time and I was so grateful for her.

He would continually put me down saying how fat I was naked, asking if he would catch something from me as I was a whore. When Jack and I initially separated a family friend of his cousin contacted me asking me to arrange a golf trip with Jack and his father, I informed him I had separated from Jack and he would need to contact him instead. He told me he had recently separated from his wife and we began chatting and from there we began dating.

It was nice to have the attention it made me feel good about myself. He would buy me gifts and take me on trips. It was nice to be wanted. However it turned out this 'nice guy' act was just that an act. I later found out he was in fact happily married with two children of which one was a new baby.

When Jack found out about this, he was furious, calling me a slag, saying I was having an affair and that I was apparently so desperate I would shag anything.

I finally broke down to my friend Jason Barratt who had recently come back in to my life. I had been holding things together for so long, telling him I was living a good life when it all just came pouring out, he knew me well and could tell things were not good. Without hesitation, he helped me out financially. I couldn't believe his kindness and generosity.

This meant I could feed my daughter, I could get my daughter Christmas presents, we could have a turkey and all the trimmings on Christmas day. I couldn't thank him enough and all he wanted in return was for me to get back on my feet, back to the Helen he once knew.

Christmas Day came and my daughter was very excited, Jack came around and our daughter opened her presents, she was having a lovely morning, Jack decided he wanted to go upstairs to sleep for a while. While Jack slept for a few hours I put the turkey in the oven and enjoyed the morning helping my daughter build her toys. Jack's mum, Dad and sister arrived. I didn't actually know they were coming as Jack invited them to see our daughter and give her presents. To say it was awkward is an understatement. I didn't want Jane in my house, but it was Christmas Day and I didn't want to spoil it for my daughter she always came first.

Whilst they were there my mobile froze and I asked Jack if he could take the photographs as my phone wasn't working. Before long, his family left, and I went into the kitchen to check on dinner. When I came back in to the living room to get my mobile, it wasn't there so I asked my daughter if she had taken it. She told me Daddy had taken my phone. I shouted to Jack who confirmed he had my phone and was trying to fix it for me.

Nova was happily playing on the floor with her new toys when Jack came down stairs, it was evident he was in a foul mood and he threw my mobile at me.

"What was that for?" I said shocked.

"You are still seeing him aren't you?" he snapped furiously.

"Who?" I asked.

. . .

"Albert" he said.

"No, I am not, I haven't seen or heard from him in a while" I said shocked at his sudden and abrupt accusations.

Jack then tried to grab hold of my phone, but I wouldn't give it to him, so he grabbed hold of me, hit me in the chest causing me to fall backwards onto the sofa then pinned me to the sofa trying to take my phone from my hand. I could barely breathe; he was shouting a barrage of abuse at me but all I could hear was my daughter screaming for Daddy to stop. For Daddy to stop hurting mummy. I'll never forget the sound of her screams.

He finally relented and let me go. I grabbed hold of my petrified, sobbing three year old daughter who had tears rolling down her face and I held her so tight. This is not the environment I want my daughter raised. He grabbed hold of her, pulling her away from me. And he told me I was an unfit mother and she would be going to his mums with him. I tried to remain calm for my daughter's sake, but I've never felt the feeling I had inside me in that moment before a mixture of anger, fear, rage, anxiety all rolled in to one. I just wanted my daughter back in my arms. I told him I needed her back and I couldn't do this anymore, we were done.

He told me to kill myself, because I was just as worthless

THE TRUTH BEHIND THE UNIFORM

and pathetic as the rest of my family, he was embarrassed to ever have been with me and that he was going back to his mums and taking our daughter with him. She was hysterical, reaching her arms out for me and screaming "Mummy, Mummy!" I told him to give her back to me. But he knew she was my weakness; she was the way he could hurt me more than anything else. She broke free and ran to me, I grabbed hold of her and screamed at Jack to get the fuck out of my house, I was so angry I slammed the door behind him. I carried my daughter back into the living room where I held on to her so tightly whilst we both cried. I told her everything was going to be ok; she was with mummy now. She was safe.

I tired to salvage what was left of Christmas Day, but the turkey had burnt, and I was looking forward to the day being over. It was the worst Christmas Day of my life and I've had some pretty shit ones. Nova was inseparable from me for the rest of the day, and me her to be honest, so we cuddled on the sofa watching Christmas movies and eating chocolate. Though I knew once Christmas was over, I would be filing for divorce in January.

The following day, there was a knock at the door, it was my neighbour Suzanne and her daughter Amelia who was the same age as Nova. I had met Suzanne once before whilst my daughter and I were walking our dog ,George, The first thing Nova said to her when we first met her was "My mummy doesn't love my Daddy anymore, he isn't very nice to my mummy and he makes her cry." I wanted the floor to open up and swallow me, but she was lovely about it.

Suzanne handed me a bottle of prosecco and a gift for Nova. I really wasn't in the mood for guests but I invited them in. Suzanne was upfront and honest, she told me she had witnessed what had happened yesterday on Christmas Day and she was about to phone the police when Jack left. She wanted to check Nova and I were ok, with that I burst out crying and told her everything, from that moment Suzanne has been one of the best and most supportive friends a person could wish for, an incredible cook so she ensured Nova and I always had a place to go for food or would happily cook extra and drop food round for us.

Suzanne and her husband would regularly see me on my sofa in my winter coat, I did this to keep warm whilst Nova wasn't home as I couldn't afford to heat the house when she wasn't there, hell I couldn't afford to heat the house when she was there, but I would always make sure it was warm when Nova was home. So, for my birthday Suzanne bought me the fluffiest, warmest blanket you could have ever wanted and when Nova was not home, I would wrap myself in the blanket over my coat. It was so warm, and I was so grateful.

Due to the assault before my wedding I was suffering with hemiplegic migraines and constant pain in my right side of head and face which I later found out is hemicranial continua headache disorder. They are extremely debilitating, but I have learned to live with them. Stress, diet, lack of sleep can impact the severity of them so I try as best I can to keep those things under control, however there are many unknown triggers that can cause an attack.

I was continuing with my employment tribunal against the police force, I would have times when I was exhausted with the fight, the stress was causing me to have more attacks and the constant paperwork and communication with my lawyer, I wondered if it would all be worth it.

Would anyone believe me, the police have a way of making people back out, of covering the truth up, the last thing they want is the public perception of them to be a negative one, especially by one of their own. I had colleagues contacting me telling me they were suffering similar mistreatment and they didn't know what to do.

I advised them of the lawyer I was dealing with but they were too scared, I was met with constant comments of "Look how they are treating you", "They are slowly destroying you Helen", "I can't afford to have zero pay, I'll lose my house" people are scared to take the police on, police officers who are mistreated are also scared to take the police force on, to challenge the way we are treated, fearful of any repercussions and name smearing. I was too but they pushed me to a point where I had nothing else to lose, it as just me and my daughter, I was backed so far into a corner the only way out was to fight, to fight for what I believed in.

The police were aware of my medical conditions and were informed that due to my medical conditions they needed to give me advanced notice, a minimum 48 hours' notice should they need to attend my home address, this is so the stress of an unexpected visit didn't set of an attack, but so I could also put in place any support I needed during the meeting.

However, on numerous occasions they turned up at my address unannounced causing numerous hemiplegic attacks and they acted oblivious. They did this as a form of intimidation and bullying. They couldn't even turn up at my correct address on one occasion despite the force being updated with the change months earlier, that tells you the level of incompetence they have with communication.

My federation representative Alan who is also a police officer and supposed to be impartial and represent the officer, yet the fact he was a police officer gave him no impartiality and is completely controlled by the police force despite making you think otherwise. He arranged to come to my house to assist me yet when he turned up all he could do was advise me to resign, apparently that was the best result for everyone, more like the best result for the police force, when I told him it wasn't the best result for me, he tried making me feel guilty about causing all the stress to my daughter, again I refused and demanded to talk to the civilian federation officer Larry who was the head of the department. On speaking with Larry, he agreed we had a great case and I should stick with it and I did. Alan's parting words were;

"I'll leave the resignation paperwork here for you, have a think about what you are doing, you'll realise its best to resign", and with that I told him to take them with him and closed the door in his face, from that point on I only dealt with my lawyer or Larry.

Maybe the police force had control over Alan because he was caught soliciting a prostitute in a police vehicle whilst on duty for personal gratification, who knows.

With the help of my friends, I started to rebuild my life, and after nine months my divorce finally came though, it was a quick divorce because I didn't want anything from him, I just wanted to close that chapter and move on, though it was a feeling of mixed emotions, I was glad to be divorced from Jack, but I also felt like I failed, I never took marriage lightly and never envisioned getting divorced.

However here I was, a single mother, a divorcee and though still technically employed by the police force, I was on zero pay, so I had to claim benefits in order to survive and put food on the table for my daughter and I. But with the help and support of a handful of friends both new and old, I slowly but surely began to get stronger, Jack continued to be Jack, abusive, but he had lost the control over me, it didn't work anymore. So, he decided to tell me he had started dating someone but he didn't get the reaction he wanted when I congratulated him, turns out he was dating her whilst we were still together but I wished them nothing but happiness. I can't and don't regret my marriage, as Jack gave me the greatest gift in my daughter Nova and for that I will always be thankful.

It took me a while but I started going back to the gym, getting both my physical and mental health back, it's not easy, and if you have ever suffered with mental illness of any sort, you will understand me when I say it's a daily battle, sometimes hourly battle, and on some days it gets the better of me, but I look back at what I have already overcome and although I am not invincible, I know no matter what life throws my way, I have the ability to overcome it.

I knew I still wanted to do something with my life, so I decided to go to university and studied abuse studies, this was the starting block for a complete life turn around.

With the encouragement of friends, I reluctantly started dating, though it was difficult being a single parent with little to no support, I decided to start online dating. I actually preferred it as I could weed out the bad apples right from the get go, then I came across a picture of a handsome man named Alexander, with gorgeous brown eyes and lovely smile I hit the "Smile" button and before long we got chatting and arranged our first date, I remember being sat in my car on the phone to my best friend Jo, nervous about meeting him when I saw him walk past the back of my car, he was more handsome in real life. We soon arranged our second and third dates and it turned out he was a wonderful man; I was completely honest with him about everything from the start and not once did I feel judged.

We took things slowly for months, then on a date I saw the kindness of his heart when we encountered a homeless gentleman, I knew then, I had fallen in love with this man. Though it was quite a while longer before I introduced Alexander and Nova, we both wanted to make sure it was long term before we made that huge step, Nova had already had so much change in her life, although when I finally did, it went really well.

I was continuing with the employment tribunal and my ill health retirement application, I had been to see a force appointed specialist Dr in relation to the ill health retirement and she fully supported my application which was fantastic news, and the employment tribunal hearing date had also been set for a four week trial to start in late January, I couldn't believe it was a four week trial, the force was calling a ridiculous amount of witnesses, my lawyer said it was intimidation tactics which I had no doubt it was.

. . .

I had to try and arrange child care for my daughter for four weeks as I would never have been home from Manchester in time to collect my daughter from school and wouldn't be able to drop her off at school in the morning, the logistical dynamics were a nightmare, Nova's Dad refused to help so my friend Suzanne said she would take care of her for me, it was a relief. Though the financial burden a four week trial was going to have on me was daunting, the fuel and car parking alone would cost me hundreds of pounds and I was still on benefits.

Then with weeks to go before the start of my employment tribunal the police force propositioned my lawyer with an offer to settle outside of court. I was incredibly mixed with emotions, if I accepted this whole ordeal would finally be over and I would finally be able to close that chapter and be rid of the police force, however, if I continued to go ahead with the trial, although we had the evidence to win, a four week trial when I still wasn't in the strongest of places mentally, reliving everything they had put me through wasn't something I was looking forward to, I had made so much progress both mentally and physically and I didn't want to take any steps backwards, not only that, I was broke, it wasn't just me, I had a daughter, I needed to think about her, she was my priority, so after discussing it with close friends, I decided even though I hadn't got a ruling of guilty they knew they had lost and I would not be another bug they could squash, so I accepted the settlement knowing I had won, I had endured everything they threw at me and I was still standing.

. . .

The feeling of knowing the whole ordeal was over was immense, that feeling alone was worth more than any settlement figure I could have received, I never had to speak or see any of them again. I couldn't thank my lawyer enough for all the hard work she'd put in and the faith and belief she had in me.

RISING FROM THE ASHES

On the 24th December 2016, I woke up a civilian for the first time in my adult life, it was a great Christmas present, to know I had officially retired, hung up my handcuffs and to be free of the toxicity of the police force was both amazing and sad. I loved the foundations and fundamental role of being a police officer, my passion was and still is to help and inspire people, however, now I choose to do so in a different role and one that is more conducive to a family life and both my mental and physical wellbeing.

They sent me a letter thanking me for my service and asking me to attend a ceremony along with other newly retired officers, needless to say I didn't go and have no intention to ever go back into a police station, they have however since sent me three copies of the official secrets act which made me chuckle.

. . .

My relationship with Alexander was going from strength to strength so we decided to try and add another little blessing to our family, we were elated when we found out I was pregnant, and it was within days of Alexanders birthday, though we were immediately met with worrying times, when I began bleeding, a hospital visit was required, thankfully after a few weeks we were ensured the pregnancy was viable.

Because of my history with miscarriages and the illness Nova suffered with when born, I was under the care of a specialist to monitor the baby, though things were always great. Both Nova and Alexander wanted to find out if we were having a little girl or boy, so when we found out we were being blessed with another little girl we were thrilled, though Nova was a little disappointed at first asking if we could throw her away and start again as she really wanted a brother, but she soon came round to having a sister when we said she can help name her.

The pregnancy was stressful, I was in the final stages of my degree, I was suffering from immense pain from SPD again and I was having more hemiplegic migraine attacks and to top it off I was the size of a whale, I could barely walk. We decided to move and renovate a house, I had numerous assignments to hand in and unfortunately missed a deadline as on the 25th April 2018 I gave birth to our beautiful second daughter Evelyn Nyra, she was absolutely perfect, Alexander was besotted and Nova completely smitten being a big sister. What better excuse for missing a deadline though, despite this I managed to graduate with an upper class 2:1, I was a little disappointed I didn't get my first, but I was elated I had completed my degree.

Because I had the surgery to remove all the ducts from my breasts, I was unable to breastfeed Evelyn, something that broke my heart as I was able to breast feed my Nova, so with full support from my Dr I applied for funding for donor breast milk, I was devastated when they denied my application as they stated my circumstances were not special enough and there is no evidence to support breast-milk is the best for baby, I shit you not, they have a massive campaign trying to get women to breast feed their babies and when a woman is unable to do so due to medical reasons, they don't want to fund the donor milk because it's expensive.

My Dr and infant feeding team were livid. Because of this I contacted every milk bank and charity in the country to try and give my daughter the best start in life. I was constantly refused due to criteria. However I was a mummy on a mission, one milk bank understood my circumstances and agreed to provide me with five to six weeks worth of breast milk, I was elated, my daughter will get some breast milk. However, the milk soon ran out and they didn't have the funding to provide me with more, breast milk is incredibly expensive, I cried the day I put Evelyn on formula but formula it had to be.

. . .

After a day or two Evelyn was struggling with her feeds, extremely gassy, lots of tummy pain and griping, being sick, having reflux and flared up with eczema. I knew right away she had an allergy to milk as Nova had the same symptoms when she started solid foods. So, I made an appointment with the Dr, as they have to follow strict government guidelines, they refused to treat Evelyn for lactose/milk allergy and insisted on her being treated for reflux only, despite all of the other symptoms. I told them all of the above but nothing I said could change their minds, they had to follow procedure, as it's a money saving procedure yet agreed it sounded like Evelyn was lactose/milk intolerant. Yes, a baby's health comes after money saving methods.

We treated her for reflux, needless to say it didn't work so we changed her formula to lactose free, it relieved a lot of symptoms however posed more, Evelyn started to have white, mucus poops all she was doing was pooping mucus and blood which as you can imagine scared the life out of me.

We phoned the brilliant 111 advice line who advised Evelyn needed to go straight to hospital.

At the hospital aside from the fact people were on beds lined in the hallway as there were no cubicles Evelynilable and lack of staff to see patients. We were seen relatively quickly.

. . .

The Drs and nurses at the hospital were once again amazing and after they got past cooing over Evelyn giving them huge smiles, they agreed that Evelyn has CMA (Cow's Milk Allergy) and the milk has caused irritation and possible damage to her digestive system and needed to be referred to a paediatric specialist to assist.

As you can imagine, it broke my heart that our daughter was/is poorly because I am not able to give her breast milk and this matter could have been avoided or at least delayed until she was old enough to tell us of her symptoms if they provided donor milk for her.

If I could afford to purchase breast donor milk I would, but it costs thousands and I physically can't afford that so now at such a young age our daughter will be having to have a chemically engineered formula. Until she is old enough to be off formula. My heart broke. Then a friend of mine told me about an incredible site on face book where mothers donate their breast milk for people like myself and Evelyn, I quickly joined and shared my story and the number of women that offered to donate milk was incredible, many women having special diets for their own children with allergies.

Many of these amazing ladies donate to milk banks so have had all the relevant medical check and provide the documentation for you to see. So, the next day I drove a few hundred miles and collected a donation from a wonderful lady who had dairy free milk. It was like gold, precious cargo. As soon as I got home and defrosted some milk and fed it to my daughter, she devoured the whole bottle, over night her symptoms reduced and she was back to normal with in 24 hours, though the eczema took a few days to clear up. So, for the last 11 months Alexander and I have been driving the length and breadth of the country collecting donor milk from some amazing women. We must have done nearly 2000 miles and spent a considerable number of hours in the car, but that's the love of a parent.

When my graduation ceremony came round it was one of the proudest moments of my life, to have both of my daughters and my wonderful man in the audience as I walked across that stage was a feeling I will never forget, to see Nova standing and waving at me as I walked across stage, so incredibly proud of her mummy, made all the late nights and early mornings writing my assignments worthwhile. She later told me she was so proud of me and she wanted to be just like mummy when she was older and also go to university. My heart filled with pride and my eyes with tears.

Since I divorced and retired from the police force I have gone from strength to strength, along with graduating from university with a bachelor's degree in abuse studies, I have gained diplomas in life coaching and CBT therapy, I have become a bestselling author, an international speaker on influencing people and motivational speaking.

. . .

I have started a business using all of my skills gained from the police and various qualifications, developed a course on effective communication and how to influence people. I have worked hard and created a bright future, I am the happiest I have ever been, I have a wonderful man who supports me and loves me unconditionally, but most importantly I have two beautiful daughters who have a healthy mummy, who I want to show that no matter what you face in life, you have the ability to overcome it and create that successful future. I want to be their inspiration, and if I can inspire others along the way, then that will be an incredible bonus.

For me, the key is to look to the future and not live in the past, if you do, you will be caught in a vicious cycle of victim mentality and self-sabotage, so don't be a hostage of your situation, turn it into a weapon, because you can't change the past, but you can create the future you want, because life is too short to settle for anything less than happiness.

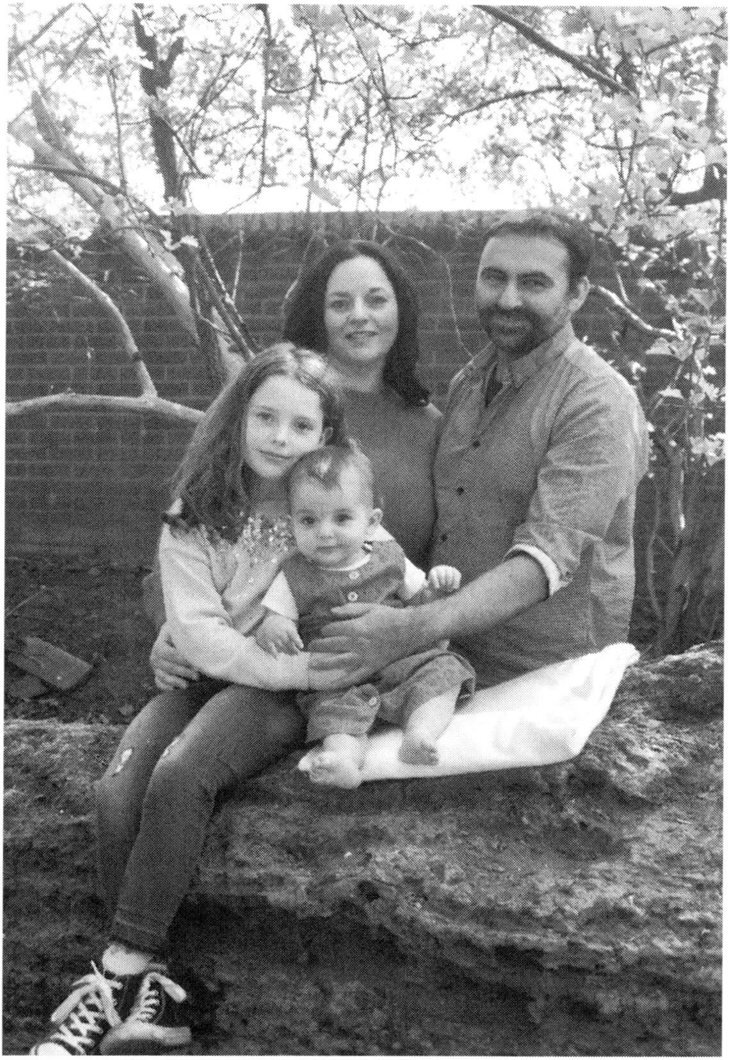

ABOUT THE AUTHOR

HELEN ELIZABETH

Bestselling author of The Woman I'm Becoming, Lifestyle Coach, Communication and influencing coach, Motivational speaker, Featured journalist on divorcedmoms.com and has been publish by the Huffington post.

Co-author of "When She Rises" to be released in June 2019

Helen is 37 years old and mother to her two girls ages seven years and eleven months. She currently resides in Cheshire with her partner, two girls and family dog George. After 14 years as a police officer Helen recently retired.

Since retiring, Helen has completed a BA Hons in abuse Studies at Manchester University and also has a Diploma in Cognitive Behavioural Therapy and a Diploma in Life Coaching. As a youth Helen played volleyball, representing England on the international scene until joining the police at 21.

Helen is passionate about her daughters, determined to provide them the family life and love which she sadly missed out on in her childhood.

She is committed to social justice, after experiencing sexism and discrimination during her career as a police officer, leading her to an employment tribunal case, as well as witnessing some of the injustices and tragedies to befall the less fortunate in society. She is an avid writer and hopes to further develop her career as an author and motivational speaker.

In sharing her message Helen hope that she can provide inspiration and positive guidance to help people realise their true potential.

To contact Helen please e.mail

hellohelenelizabeth@outlook.com

facebook.com/HelenElizabethAuthor
instagram.com/HelenElizabethAuthor

ACKNOWLEDGMENTS

Photographs by Jenine Taylor photography Bolton

www.jeninetaylorphotography.co.uk

Printed in Great Britain
by Amazon